100
THINGS TO
KNOW ABOUT
THE
UNKNOWN

Usborne Quicklinks

For links to websites and videos where you can delve into many
of the facts described in this book and explore unexplained events,
unusual wildlife and much more, go to **usborne.com/Quicklinks**
and type in the keywords: **things to know about the unknown**.

Here are some of the things you can do at the websites we recommend:

- Venture into a forest after dark to spot glowing ghost mushrooms.
- Explore mysteries surrounding the Great Sphinx of Giza.
- Find out why scientists are excited about soil.
- Look at the past, present and future of predicting earthquakes.
- See Anne Frank's diary and her family's hiding place during the Second World War.

Please follow the online safety guidelines at Usborne Quicklinks.
Children should be supervised online.

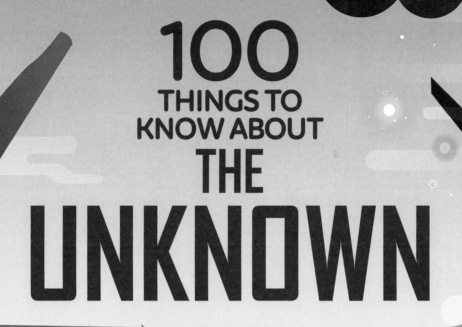

100
THINGS TO
KNOW ABOUT
THE
UNKNOWN

Written by
Jerome Martin, Alice James,
Micaela Tapsell and Alex Frith

Illustrated by
Federico Mariani, Shaw Nielsen,
Dominique Byron and Geraldine Sy

Designed by
Jenny Offley, Lenka Jones
and Tom Ashton-Booth

What is there to know about the unknown?

Actually, there's a *lot* to know. The unknown is really just the next in a long series of human explorations, inventions and discoveries. In this book you'll find a hundred facts about the world's most interesting unanswered questions.

For example, what is the universe made of?

And how fast could a *T. rex* really run?

There are many different kinds of unknowns.
These are just a few:

Things that are still awaiting discovery...

Things we *think* are true — but that we can't know for sure...

Things that can *never* be known...

Things that *somebody* knows — but that they're not telling...

Things we could know if only we were *allowed* to find them out...

Things that people once knew — but that now *nobody* knows...

Things that we're all better off *not* knowing...

Things we don't even *know* we don't know...

The boundary between the known and the unknown is moving all the time.

Scientists, mathematicians, historians and philosophers are constantly making new discoveries, solving riddles and proving (or disproving) theories.

In fact, some of the mysteries in this book may be solved by the time you read it.

Others may *never* be solved. And — who knows — some day, you might solve one yourself!

But don't worry — we'll never run out of unknowns. The more we know, the more we know there's more to know.

For a list of interesting and difficult terms, go to the glossary on pages 124-125.

1 All the planets spin...

but Venus twirls to a different tune.

As they orbit the Sun, the eight planets in the solar system also spin. *Most* of them spin in the same direction... but Venus is different.

Each planet spins around an imaginary line through its middle, called its **axis**.

Axis

Almost every planet spins around its axis in this direction, known as **prograde**.

Jupiter

Mars

Saturn

Uranus

This planet was knocked onto its side long ago – but still spins in the same direction.

Earth

Venus

Unlike the rest, Venus spins very slowly in what appears to be the *opposite* direction, described as **retrograde**.

Mercury

Neptune

No one knows *why* this is, but astronomers have come up with two possible explanations:

1

The flip
Long ago, Venus was hit by one or more big asteroids. It kept on spinning, but the impact flipped the planet upside down.

2

The reverse
Over millions of years, the Sun's powerful gravity pulled on Venus's thick atmosphere. This created strong forces, like a tide, that slowed and finally reversed the planet's spin.

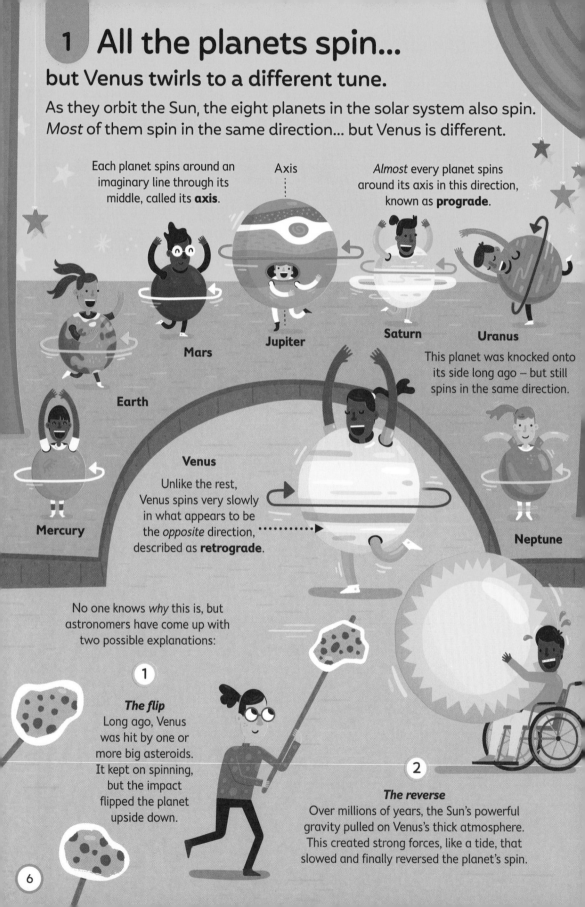

2 Chimps can chat...

but they can't ask questions.

Some chimps and gorillas have been taught to communicate through sign language. They can chat, but don't ever ask questions. It seems that they have no concept that there might be anything they don't know...

Children, chimps and gorillas all have similarly sized brains. Young children ask questions all the time – that's how they learn.

Chimps and gorillas, on the other hand, only ever make statements.

Where do we get more food?

Food. You have food.

Why don't you have food?

There are berries there.

Should we share the food?

I want food. I'm hungry.

Why are some berries red?

...

Scientists wonder if being able to ask questions – and having a concept of the *unknown* – is what sets humans apart from other apes.

3 X marks the unknown...

from maps to mathematics.

It can be hard to write about, talk about or investigate something that's unknown or uncertain. Sometimes, it helps to give the unknown a name, and often people call it **X**.

X in algebra

In a type of mathematics called algebra, x stands for any unknown value.

Mathematicians can then use equations to try to figure out what x is.

$$ax^2+bx+c=0$$

$$\log xy = \log x + \log y$$

X-ray

The X in X-rays stands for unknown radiation. When scientists first discovered it, they didn't know what it was. Today they know it's electromagnetic radiation, but the name has stuck.

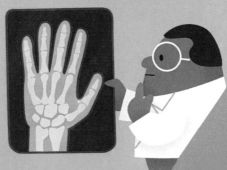

X mark

In the past, the majority of people never learned to read or write. They couldn't sign important documents...

Important Document

Signed X

...so they used an X instead, known as an X mark. The real names of these people have been lost.

X marks the spot

In stories, X is often used on a map to mark the spot where hidden treasure might lie.

Malcolm X

Malcolm X was an activist and religious leader, who stood up for African Americans in the US during the 1950s and 60s.

He used X to represent his unknown African name. For over 400 years, millions of Africans were taken to America and the Caribbean, given new names and forced to work as slaves. As a result, many African Americans don't know their ancestral names.

X-Planes

Since the 1940s, the US has been building a series of experimental aircraft. Their names all begin with the letter X. These planes, many of them top-secret, try out new, cutting-edge technologies.

4 The most confusing snail...
had 113 names.

When a completely unique type of living thing is discovered, scientists call it a new **species**. They identify it, describe it, and give it an official name, which is usually in Latin. That way, all scientists know what it is.

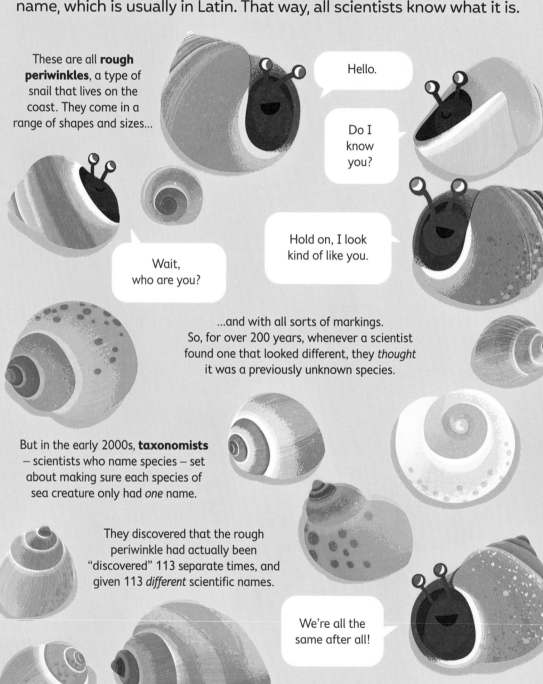

These are all **rough periwinkles**, a type of snail that lives on the coast. They come in a range of shapes and sizes...

Hello.

Do I know you?

Hold on, I look kind of like you.

Wait, who are you?

...and with all sorts of markings. So, for over 200 years, whenever a scientist found one that looked different, they *thought* it was a previously unknown species.

But in the early 2000s, **taxonomists** – scientists who name species – set about making sure each species of sea creature only had *one* name.

They discovered that the rough periwinkle had actually been "discovered" 113 separate times, and given 113 *different* scientific names.

We're all the same after all!

Now they all go by a single scientific name: *Littorina saxatilis*.

5 Yetis definitely don't exist...

unless they definitely do.

In 1951, a British explorer photographed a huge ape-like footprint in the snow on Mount Everest. Some people believed the mark had been left by an enormous, muscular ice-creature said to prowl the mountains...

A few years later, a team of 500 people spent six months scouring the Himalayan mountains for proof of the yeti. They came back empty-handed.

But the ancient folklore of the Himalayan people insists that a dangerous bear-man *does* exist, and it roams where few ever venture.

In 2017, scientists tested the DNA of supposed yeti samples that had been collected over the years, including bones and hair. They found that *all* the samples came from known species – mostly bears.

But many people are still finding new signs, from footprints in the snow to sightings of a bear-man roaming the land. Today, the search for the yeti continues...

There's no way to predict...

when an earthquake will hit – yet.

Earthquakes happen when places deep underground start to shake. A major quake can cause catastrophic damage above ground. If we could forecast them as accurately as rain, many lives could be saved.

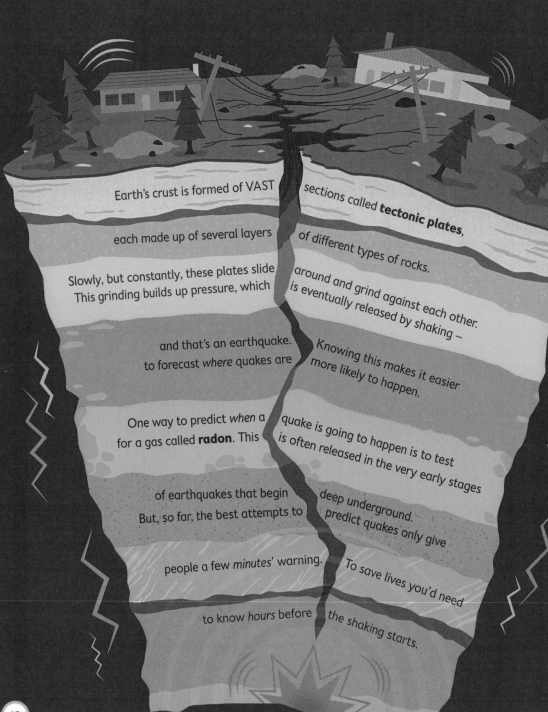

Earth's crust is formed of VAST sections called **tectonic plates**,

each made up of several layers of different types of rocks.

Slowly, but constantly, these plates slide around and grind against each other. This grinding builds up pressure, which is eventually released by shaking –

and that's an earthquake. Knowing this makes it easier to forecast where quakes are more likely to happen.

One way to predict when a quake is going to happen is to test for a gas called **radon**. This is often released in the very early stages

of earthquakes that begin deep underground. But, so far, the best attempts to predict quakes only give

people a few *minutes'* warning. To save lives you'd need

to know *hours* before the shaking starts.

7 You can be famous...

but still be anonymous, if you're pseudonymous.

Some people are world-famous, but are only known by a
pseudonym – a false name. To the world at large, their true
names are unknown, making them **anonymous**.

"Elena Ferrante" is an Italian novelist
who doesn't want readers to be distracted
by her identity. "For those who love
literature, the books are enough," she says.

"El Shaheed" are protestors in
Egypt who hid their identities to avoid
being arrested by the government
they were protesting against.

"The Stig" is a stunt driver
on a TV show in the UK.
By staying anonymous,
multiple drivers can do the job.

"Satoshi Nakamoto" is the
creator of a new type of currency
known as Bitcoin. They do not
want to be interviewed.

"The Residents" are a US art-rock band
formed in the 1960s. They wear disguises,
so that their fans can focus on the
music, not the musicians.

"Banksy" is a British artist known
for painting, in secret, on public
walls. Technically this is illegal,
so he remains pseudonymous.

8 Magic mud...

is baseball's best-kept secret.

Before professional baseball games, players tend to cover shiny new balls in mud to improve their grip. But muddy balls are hard to spot in the air, so one family in the US found a solution: vanishing mud.

For generations, the same family has collected mud from a secret location along the Delaware River. They sell it to teams, who smear it on the baseballs before big games.

Unlike every other kind of mud, this Delaware dirt fades when it dries, so that balls *appear* white, but have optimum grip.

To this day, chemists and engineers have not been able to replicate this mud's ideal ball-coating qualities.

According to the official rulebook for Major League Baseball, this magic mud is the *only* substance allowed on the roughly 300,000 balls used in games every season.

9 Your dreams begin...

somewhere scientists can't find.

Dreams have been a source of fascination for thousands of years, but **oneirologists** – scientists who study dreams – still have some very big, unanswered questions.

Oneirologists can track the electrical activity in volunteers' brains while they sleep. Their studies show that people generally dream several times a night.

Dreams typically last under 20 minutes, even if they feel as though they last all night.

When?

Most dreams happen during a part of sleep called **REM** (short for rapid eye movement) when your brain is buzzing with activity and your eyes are darting around beneath your eyelids.

Where?

Brain data and electrical signals give *some* clues to oneirologists trying to locate where in the brain dreams begin. But so far, they don't know whether they're looking for *one* or *several* sources.

Why?

All this research has led to lots of theories about why we dream, but scientists have yet to find a definitive answer.

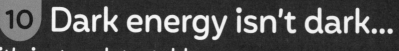

10 Dark energy isn't dark...

it's just undetectable.

The universe is expanding. Not just expanding gently, but more and more rapidly all the time. According to physicists, this shouldn't be possible, *without some source of energy*. They call this unknown source **dark energy**.

Hey, *you're* all astronomers and physicists... so tell me – what actually *is* it?

Not a clue. It's a mystery. It's neither light nor dark... we can't see it, or hear it, or smell it, or feel it.

But we *can* see its *effect* in the universe. *Something* is pushing galaxies and stars and space itself further and faster apart.

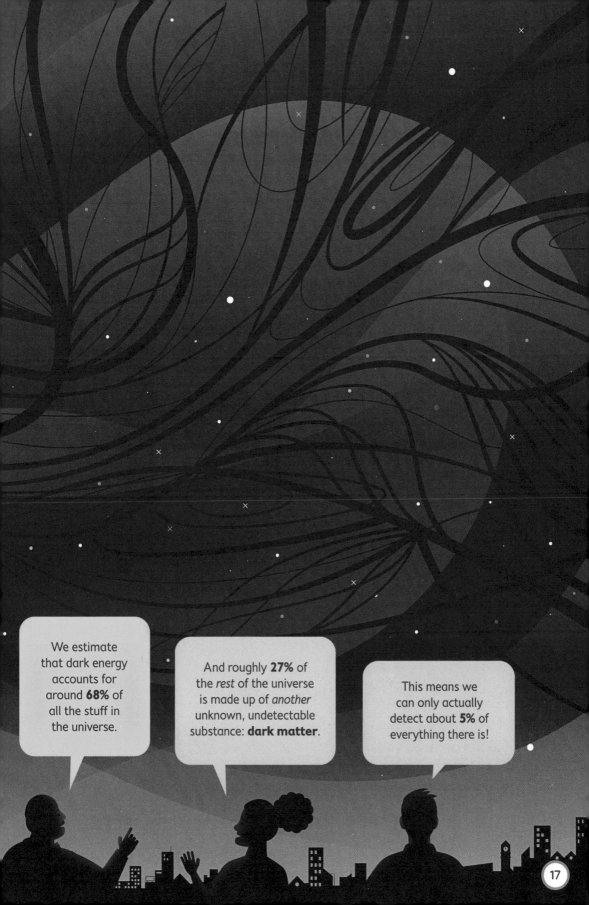

11 The longest river...

is only as long as people *say* it is.

Rivers are measured from their source to their mouth. Locating the mouth is usually easy – it's where the river joins the sea or a lake. But finding the source is trickier...

If you follow the course of a river back from its mouth, you'll find other rivers flow into it.

A big river has a branching structure, like a tree. You'll have to choose between different routes to follow.

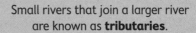

Small rivers that join a larger river are known as **tributaries**.

12 One winning Olympian...

has never been named.

At the 1900 Paris Olympic Games, a young boy was picked from the crowd to join a rowing event. His team won, but the boy left before he could receive his award. Even today, nobody knows who he was.

Rowers in this competition rely on a teammate called a **cox** to steer the boat and keep the rowers in time. The lighter the cox, the faster the rowers can go.

The Dutch team had struggled in previous races. Minutes before the final event, they swapped their heavy cox with a small child from the crowd.

The total length of the river depends on *which* tributaries you follow...

...whether you measure up the middle of the water, or along the banks...

...and how closely you measure each bend.

Mapmakers agree that there are two contenders for the world's longest river, but disagree on how long they are.

The **Amazon**, in South America, is measured as anything from
6,275km (3,899 miles)
to
6,992km (4,345 miles).

The **Nile**, in Africa, is measured as anything from
5,499km (3,417 miles)
to
7,088km (4,404 miles).

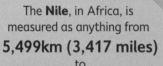

This last-minute decision won them the race.

The three unlikely team members took a photo together, which remains the only clue of the boy's identity.

13 The Great Sphinx of Giza...

may not actually be a sphinx.

Resting beside the Great Pyramid in Giza, Egypt, is an enormous statue known today as the Great Sphinx. It is named after a mythical creature – but what is it *really*? While archaeologists know a lot about it, many questions remain, for which we can only *imagine* the answers.

The statue was probably built 4,500 years ago. But archaeologists don't know for sure *who* built it, nor *why*, nor even *what* it's meant to be.

2,500 years ago, some ancient Greek writers gave it the name **sphinx**, because it looks a little like the sphinx from Greek mythology: a creature with a human head, lion's body and eagle's wings.

But local people don't call it a sphinx. Today, Egyptians call it *Abu al-Hawl*, which means *Father of Terror*.

Did the statue once have wings? Is it really a sphinx? We don't know.

Whose face features on the statue? No one knows *for sure* – but centuries ago, someone climbed up and hacked its nose off. *Who* did it, and *why*? We don't know.

Archaeologists don't even think the face carved on the Sphinx is part of its *original* design. They think this one was added later.

Who did the Sphinx's *original* face look like? There are few clues left that hint at who it might have been or whether it was human or animal.

14 Women vanished from history...

because of the Matilda Effect.

For centuries, women's scientific achievements and discoveries were overlooked or even erased, and credited to men instead. In fact, it happened so much, it was given a name: the Matilda Effect.

This phenomenon was first described in the 1800s by a woman named Matilda Joslyn Gage. Over time, researchers have rediscovered some of the women whose work had been erased from the history books.

I'm Rosalind Franklin, a chemist who took the first photo of DNA. The lab I worked in even won the ultimate science award – a Nobel Prize! But I was left out, and the prize just went to the men.

I'm Alice Ball. I developed an amazing cure for leprosy. Unfortunately, when I died, my boss took all the credit for my work. It was many decades before my contribution was discovered.

I'm Trota, an Italian doctor who lived 800 years ago. I wrote many important books on medicine for women, but for centuries my name was hidden.

I'm Jocelyn Bell Burnell. I worked in a lab that discovered things in space called pulsars. But my name was left off our Nobel Prize too.

Sadly, we may never know exactly how many famous discoveries were actually made by women.

15 The universe is wonky...

when in theory it should be symmetrical.

Since people first started studying the stars, scientists have developed theories about the shape of the universe. But until recently, they haven't been able to put their theories to the test.

Most scientists think the universe started billions of years ago with an event called the **Big Bang**. At that moment, all of space expanded rapidly out of a tiny, hot, dense point.

After that, most scientists agree that the universe *should* have expanded at the same rate in all directions.

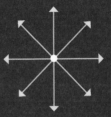

In *theory*, this means galaxies that formed should be distributed evenly on all sides.

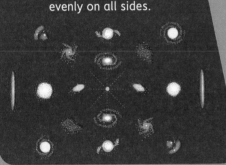

With the recent invention of powerful space telescopes, scientists have been able to study millions of galaxies over vast distances.

Their results show that the universe *appears* to be expanding faster in some directions than others. In other words, the universe could be lopsided.

We don't yet know why!

If we keep getting the same results, we will need to rethink our understanding of the universe — right from the very beginning...

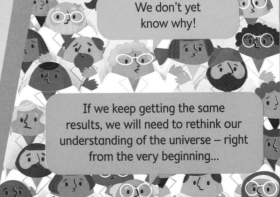

16 Crashed, kidnapped or cast away...
no one will ever know.

In the 1930s, when planes were a new and exciting technology, many pilots became famous. One of the most famous was an American woman named Amelia Earhart. She set out to be the first person to fly all the way around the world. But, somewhere over the Pacific Ocean, she disappeared.

For decades, people have been asking: **what happened to Amelia Earhart?**

Things we *know* happened

Theories about what happened

July 2nd, 1937, 10:00 am: Earhart and Noonan set off from New Guinea, heading for Howland Island.

About 20 hours later: Earhart sends her last known radio message to a coastguard in the Pacific Ocean.

Within one hour, search and rescue operations begin, but no trace of Earhart's plane is found.

Hi! I'm Amelia Earhart. That is the plane I was flying around the world, along with my navigator, Fred Noonan.

Did Earhart and Noonan die in a plane crash? Or, as some suspect, is there more to their story?

Theory 1

The plane runs out of fuel and crash lands in the Pacific Ocean. It sinks.

Theory 2

Crash landing on the tiny Pacific island of Nikumaroro. Pilot and navigator die on impact.

Theory 3

Emergency landing on Nikumaroro. Earhart and Noonan survive and live as castaways.

Theory 4

Earhart and Noonan lose their way and land on the Marshall Islands, controlled by Japan.

July 9th, 1937: A week after Earhart disappears, a US plane flies over Nikumaroro. It reports signs of habitation – on an island no one had lived on in 40 years.

At this time, Japan is a rival of the US. The Americans are mistaken for spies, taken prisoner and, eventually, they die in captivity.

It's possible that the two adventurers survive for weeks or even years on the remote island, waiting for a rescue that never comes.

January 1939: 18 months after disappearing, Earhart is officially declared dead.

1940: Someone finds human bones on Nikumaroro, at the time believed to be a man's.

1989: An official investigation suggests the bones are likely to belong to a tall woman, like Earhart.

To this day, the debate about what happened to Earhart rages on. There is not enough conclusive proof to back up or rule out any of these theories.

Since 1937, people have scoured hundreds of thousands of miles of ocean and coastline, and millions of dollars have been spent on the effort to find out what happened.

17 Crocodiles cry...

but no one knows why.

People often refer to "crocodile tears" as a way of describing false sadness or fake tears. But, as a matter of fact, crocodiles *do* shed real tears when they eat – scientists just aren't sure why.

18 A secret sauce...

can make a fortune.

Sometimes companies keep valuable information – such as inventions, ideas, or the recipe for a special sauce – hidden from the public and from rival companies. These **trade secrets** can be worth millions... as long as they are closely guarded.

But trade secrets are a risky game. People from other companies can use all kinds of sneaky tricks to try to steal secrets from their rivals...

I am going to try to get a job with the company so I can learn the secret! This is a type of spying called **industrial espionage**. It's against the law.

I'm one of the few people who knows the recipe for my company's famous sauce.

I am going to work backwards to figure out the ingredients and how it's made. This is called **reverse engineering**.

As long as a company keeps its trade secrets safe from the competition, it has a product nobody can copy – and that can be worth a fortune.

19 The end of the universe...

will come in one of *four* big varieties.

Most scientists agree that the universe *began* around fourteen billion years ago with an event called the **Big Bang**. But when it comes to the *end* of the universe, there's a variety pack of theories to choose from.

Ever since the Big Bang, the universe has been constantly expanding: its galaxies, stars and planets drifting further and further apart. How will it all end?

Scientists have four main theories:

Galactic Snax Multipack

THE BIG CHILL

GALACTIC SNAX: The snack to END all snacks

Eventually, the universe could expand so much that stars would die out, everything would become cold and there would be no movement or light anywhere ever again.

It doesn't get COOLER than this!

Galactic Snax Multipack

THE BIG RIP

GALACTIC SNAX: The snack to END all snacks

The universe could continue to expand, going faster and faster until — at some point — space itself tears apart completely and stops existing.

TEAR into a universe of taste!

Galactic Snax Multipack

THE BIG CRUNCH

GALACTIC SNAX: The snack to END all snacks

At some point, the expanding universe could go into reverse. Everything would snap back like an elastic band, crunching galaxies together into one tiny, hot, dense point.

A whole UNIVERSE in every bite!

Galactic Snax Multipack

The Big Bounce

GALACTIC SNAX: The snack to END all snacks

If the Big Crunch happens, the tiny point could become so dense that it would explode — like another Big Bang. This may have happened before, and might continue happening forever.

The snack you eat AGAIN and AGAIN and AGAIN...

Scientists are still gathering data about what the universe is made of and how it is all changing over time.

Physicists think the Big Rip and Big Chill are the most likely scenarios... but the universe probably won't end for billions, or even trillions, of years. Which gives scientists plenty of time to come up with more theories!

20 The shape of a country...

can shift with the climate.

Some borders between countries are defined by natural features such as rivers, lakes and mountains. But what happens when the climate changes – and the landscape changes with it?

Part of the border between Italy and Switzerland runs through a place called the Theodul Pass, high up in the Alps. This is how it looked some 40 years ago.

A **pass** is a low point between mountain peaks. Officially, the border follows the **watershed** of the pass – the highest part, from which water flows to one side of the mountain or the other.

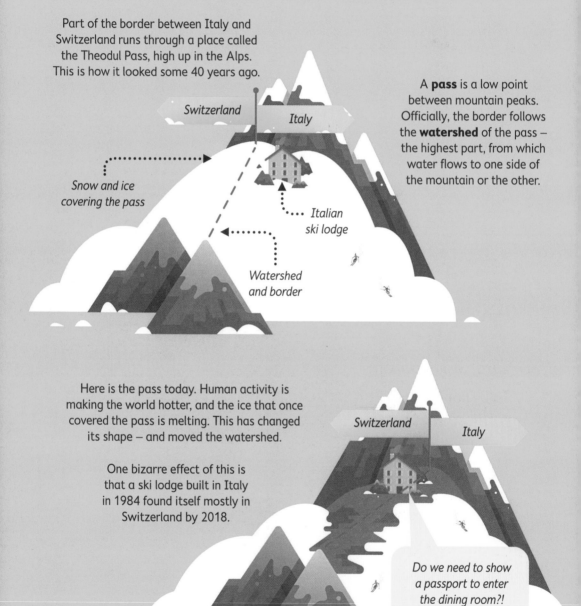

Switzerland

Italy

Snow and ice covering the pass

Italian ski lodge

Watershed and border

Here is the pass today. Human activity is making the world hotter, and the ice that once covered the pass is melting. This has changed its shape – and moved the watershed.

One bizarre effect of this is that a ski lodge built in Italy in 1984 found itself mostly in Switzerland by 2018.

Switzerland

Italy

Do we need to show a passport to enter the dining room?!

Italy and Switzerland have agreed a new border deal for the Theodul Pass. But, as temperatures rise, other mountain borders will be affected too. What once seemed fixed will shift and change in ways we can't predict.

A hypothetical cloud of ice...

is where scientists *guess* some comets are born.

A scientific guess is called a **hypothesis**. It's based on real data, but hasn't been proven yet. One such guess is about what *might* be drifting out in the coldest, darkest, furthest part of the solar system.

Astronomers hypothesize that the solar system is encircled by a vast cloud of *trillions* of chunks of ice. They call it the **Oort Cloud**.

These ice chunks would be about **20,000 times** further from the Sun than we are on Earth. Astronomers can't actually *see* them directly. They're too distant, too dim, too widely scattered.

But they *do* send visible signs of their existence.

The Oort Cloud orbits the Sun — but from time to time, the gravity of *other* nearby stars pulls a chunk of ice off course...

...and turns it into a **comet**: an icy object looping in toward the Sun, with a streaming tail of gas and dust.

The Sun

Astronomers have observed comets over centuries. They have traced their paths back through space and come up with a hypothesis.

Their calculations suggest that many comets have one most likely source: in the invisible, unimaginably distant cloud.

Dinosaur skin is a mystery...

but their feathers are full of facts.

Dinosaurs died out millions of years ago. They left behind rocky remains in the ground called **fossils**, which scientists can use to build up a picture of the dinosaur world. But *some* body parts fossilize better than others – so the picture still has gaps...

Dinosaurs' leathery **skin** usually rotted away before it could become fossilized. But there *are* lots of fossils of dinosaur **bones** and **feathers**.

In fact, feathers fossilized *so* well that they can help scientists to figure out what feathered dinos looked like.

Dinosaurs are closely related to today's birds. Scientists can compare **cells** inside bird feathers to those in dinosaur feather fossils. When they spot similar cells, they can work out the shades of a dinosaur's feathers.

Anchiornis

Sausage-shaped cells mean feathers were very dark.

Sinosauropteryx

Circular cells are likely to mean orange feathers.

Microraptor

Flattened cells are linked with metallic, shimmery feathers with a beautiful sheen.

T. rex

Because skin doesn't fossilize well, it's much harder to know the patterns and shades of dinosaurs whose fossils *don't* include feathers, such as the *T. rex*. For these dinosaurs, it's usually just scientists' best guess...

23 This ship is either old or new...

it's either one ship – or it's two.

A brain teaser that seems to contradict itself and go against logic or common sense is known as a **paradox**. In ancient Greece, philosophers came up with a paradox that still puzzles thinkers today.

It goes like this: imagine that a famous ship – called **the Ship of Theseus** – is carefully preserved for years and years.

Whenever a piece of the ship starts to wear out, we replace it with a new one.

Eventually, we swap out every sail, plank and peg. Not *one* original piece remains.

So: is the Ship of Theseus *still* the Ship of Theseus? Or is it now a new and different ship? And *if* it's a new ship, when did it *stop* being the Ship of Theseus?

But wait – what if we collected all the worn-out pieces of the original ship...

...and assembled them into a second ship. Would *this* be the real Ship of Theseus? Or would there be two?

24 A teaspoon of soil...

is packed full of hidden life.

At first glance, soil might look like a lifeless pile of dirt. But, it's actually teeming with a mind-blowing variety of living things – things we just can't see without powerful microscopes.

One teaspoon of soil can contain several miles of fungal filaments – long strands of living things called fungi...

...and more than a billion bacteria cells from as many as 100,000 different types of soil bacteria.

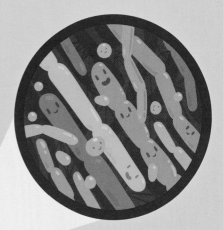

Scientists know that some soil bacteria, such as streptomyces, help crops to grow by breaking down substances in the soil.

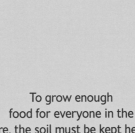

But many more soil bacteria have yet to be identified or studied in enough detail to know what benefits they might bring.

To grow enough food for everyone in the future, the soil must be kept healthy. Scientists believe the key is discovering more about these mysterious bacteria that give soil its life.

25 Blobs from outer space...

could have an earthly explanation.

One night in 1950, in the US city of Philadelphia, two police officers saw a strange shape drifting down from the sky. When they went to investigate, what they found seemed truly out of this world: a glowing, mysterious, gooey blob.

The strange blob went on to inspire both scientific investigations and a sci-fi movie.

THE ORIGINAL BLOB

See it now! The movie about the blob that inspired a movie about a blob!

IT INSPIRES!
★ ★ ★ ★ ★

It spawned a famously silly movie villain in *The Blob* in 1958!

IT GLOWS!

The blob radiates an otherworldly shade of purple!

IT SPARKLES!

It's as though it contains crystals!

IT DISSOLVES!
★ ★

When touched, it simply melts away!

It's NOT the FIRST – or LAST – of its kind! For centuries, people have recorded sightings of a substance known as **star jelly** or **astral jelly** falling from the sky.

There's no evidence that blobs such as this one actually came from space.

Scientists have many theories about what they really are – frog innards? Fungus? Fresh-water algae? But so far, none has been proven.

26 A deep space mystery...
might be solved deep underground.

Astrophysicists believe that distant galaxies *could* be held together by a puzzling substance called **dark matter**. But no one knows what it's made of, or how it works. In fact, the answer to the mystery may not be found in outer space, but in special labs built in abandoned mines.

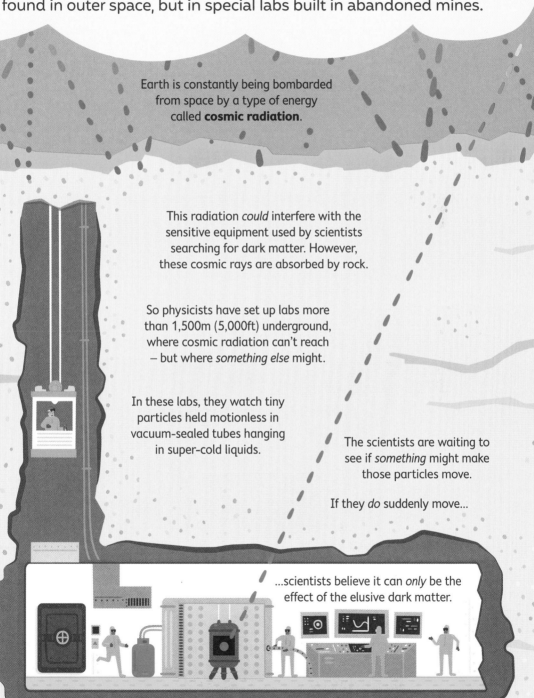

Earth is constantly being bombarded from space by a type of energy called **cosmic radiation**.

This radiation *could* interfere with the sensitive equipment used by scientists searching for dark matter. However, these cosmic rays are absorbed by rock.

So physicists have set up labs more than 1,500m (5,000ft) underground, where cosmic radiation can't reach – but where *something else* might.

In these labs, they watch tiny particles held motionless in vacuum-sealed tubes hanging in super-cold liquids.

The scientists are waiting to see if *something* might make those particles move.

If they *do* suddenly move...

...scientists believe it can *only* be the effect of the elusive dark matter.

27 Nobody knows how colossal...

the most colossal squid can be.

For centuries, sailors have told fantastic tales of huge, tentacled creatures that lurk beneath the waves. Today, we know these creatures really *do* exist. But we still don't know *how big* they can grow.

The first proof that these animals exist came in 1924, when their tentacles were found in the stomachs of deep-diving whales.

The tentacles were far bigger than those of *any* known squid, and covered in rows of hooks. Scientists examining them realized they had found a new species. They called it the **colossal squid**.

It lives in deep, pitch-black waters around Antarctica, and it took more than 50 years before a whole colossal squid was finally caught and examined.

To this day, very few have been seen in the wild.

Scientists *suspect* a colossal squid can grow longer than a bus... but they don't know for sure.

The very *biggest* colossal squids stay *miles* below the surface. Nobody has ever seen one of them, let alone measured one.

28 Empty frames hang...

at the scene of the priciest art robbery.

Early one morning in March 1990, 13 works of art were stolen from a gallery in Boston, US.

Guards at the gallery were tied up, and the works were seized by thieves pretending to be police officers.

Together, the stolen art is thought to be worth over $500 million.

One stolen work is a painting by an artist named Johannes Vermeer. Just 34 of his paintings survive today, and this is thought to be the most expensive piece of stolen art in history.

To this day, not a single one of the stolen pieces has been found. Empty frames still hang in the gallery, waiting for them to be returned.

Art experts and detectives are puzzled. Who were the thieves? Why did they steal *these* works and leave *other* valuable art behind? And where are the artworks now?

29 For every prime that we know...

there are always more that we don't.

For thousands of years, mathematicians have puzzled over a set of special numbers called **prime numbers**, or **primes**.

Any whole number that can *only* be divided by itself or 1 is known as a prime number.

Prime: ⬤   Non-prime: ⚪

| 1 | 2 | 3 | 4 | 5 | 6 | 7 | 8 | 9 | 10 |

| 11 | 12 | 13 | 14 | 15 | 16 | 17 | 18 | 19 | 20 |

Over the centuries, mathematicians have calculated the first thousand, million and even billion prime numbers...

...but no one knows if there is a method for predicting *all* prime numbers. Is there a pattern? Mathematicians have long searched for one.

Here's what happens if you arrange the numbers 1 to 1,140 as a spiral of dots, with the primes highlighted in pink.

I still can't detect a pattern here... But we'll keep trying different ways of looking at the sequence of primes. *So many* number sequences have a pattern – there must be one here too!

Oh, I can't wait for someone to find the pattern to predict prime numbers! I'm sure they'll be celebrated all around the world!

Solving the problem of primes...

could set off a cascade of crimes.

Because there is currently no way to identify all prime numbers, credit card companies use them to create secret codes that keep bank accounts safe from hackers. So, if the problem of primes is ever solved, it *might* enable thieves to commit card fraud.

> We bankers use gigantic prime numbers – with thousands of digits – to convert a credit card number into a secret code.

This is how banks do it: if you find two *big* prime numbers, then multiply them together, you get a *super big* number:

Big primes   Super big number

$125{,}243 \times 773{,}251 = 96{,}844{,}274{,}993$

This new number can *only* be divided by two numbers: the original big prime numbers.

But, if you didn't already know the original primes, it would take *ages* to figure them out. If the original primes are made of thousands of digits, it would take someone days or weeks – even *with* the help of a supercomputer.

> The only way to unlock the code – and so authorize the card for spending – is if you know the *exact* prime numbers that were used.

> Oh, I hope nobody ever finds the pattern to predict prime numbers. If they did, they could hack credit cards all around the world!

31 Strange desert circles...

spark heated debates.

In parts of the dry grasslands of Namibia, in Africa, the ground is dotted with strange patches of bare soil, known as **fairy circles**. Scientists have long debated what caused them – and even today, they still disagree.

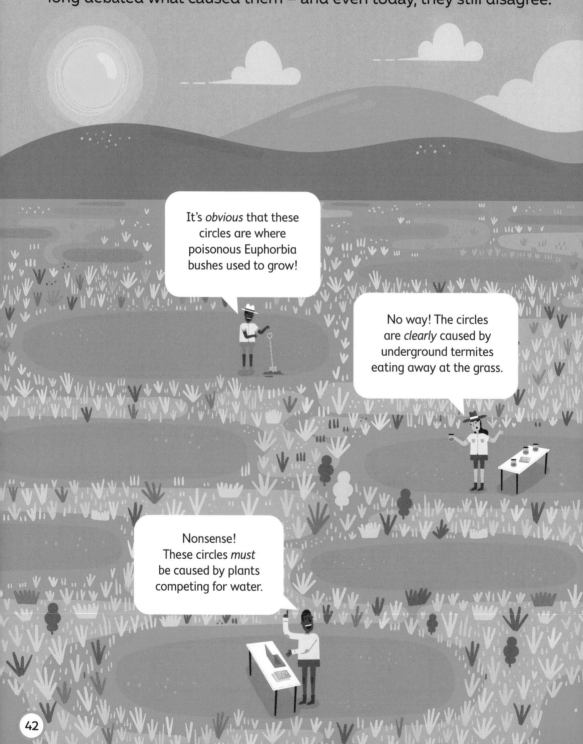

32 Fashion has forgotten...

what the bobble on a bobble hat is for.

Lots of the clothes we wear today have been around for hundreds, if not thousands, of years. Items were often designed to serve a specific function... but what was it? Often, fashion historians have *theories*, but no definite answers.

Some people *think* bobble hats were designed to protect sailors from bumping their heads on low decks.

Others *suspect* they originate from a time when soldiers wore bobbles to show their rank, or which regiment they belonged to.

The first sunglasses *might* have been used by Chinese judges around 900 years ago.

This wasn't to protect their eyes from the Sun, but to conceal their reactions in court.

Foreign soldiers fighting for France 400 years ago wore strips of cloth around their necks, *perhaps* for identification, or for warmth.

The French upper classes liked the way these troops looked, and the necktie became an item worn to show off status.

The oldest known trousers, or pants, were found in China, and are over 3,000 years old.

They were *probably* designed specifically for horse-riding, and were made from wool.

33 The ghost fungus glows...

for reasons nobody knows.

There are over 100 species of fungus that glow in the dark. For *most* species this glow, or **bioluminescence**, has a clear function.

> Scientists have found that we glow to attract insects...

> ...who pick up and spread our seed-like spores to other places where more of us can grow.

34 Answering the unanswerable...

is one path to achieving enlightenment.

Zen Buddhism is a religion, founded by a person called the Buddha. It helps people find a state of peace and understanding known as enlightenment. Achieving this often involves thinking through a series of puzzling sayings or unanswerable questions known as **koans**.

What did your face look like before your mother and father were born?

If you meet the Buddha, kill the Buddha.

Is the flag moving? Or is the wind moving?

Neither. Your *mind* is moving.

However, this is not the case with the Australian ghost fungus...

Insects don't seem to be attracted to us. So why do we glow?

Is it to warn animals and insects not to eat us?

Or is it to attract creatures that will eat the creatures that try to eat *us*?

No one really knows *why* we glow. For now, it remains a mystery!

What is Buddha? Three pounds of flax.

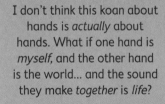

I don't think this koan about hands is *actually* about hands. What if one hand is *myself*, and the other hand is the world... and the sound they make *together* is *life*?

And what if I could make myself *one* with the world — what "sound" would that make? What would life be like then?

Two hands clap and there is a sound. What is the sound of just *one* hand?

Koans don't have a specific meaning or solution — Zen Buddhists should try to embrace what's unknowable in them.

35 An unknown intelligence lurks...

in the dusty corners of your home.

This intelligence can make plans, learn from the past and map out journeys before it takes them. And it's been doing this mostly unnoticed, just a few steps away from you. What is it? It's *spider* intelligence.

Scientists studying spiders have found they are a *lot* smarter than anyone guessed. In fact, each line of a web represents a decision a spider has made.

A spider can build webs to catch flies to eat. It plans its web based on how much silk it has left.

It can explore the space where it's going to build its web and measure the distances.

It can make a mental map of a room to find the quickest routes and avoid hazards.

It can tighten its web in places where it has caught insects before, and where they are likely to be caught again.

Intelligence is the ability to solve problems and learn from experience. Humans tend to think that only big animals – like us – have this power, but spiders are making scientists reconsider.

How many other unknown intelligences are out there?

that he can never let go.

In Florence, Italy, stands a famous sculpture of a youth known as David. He is about to go into battle against a fearsome giant, Goliath. In his left hand, he holds a leather strap. In his right hand, he holds... *something*.

This 5m (17ft) statue was carved from a single block of marble in the early 16th century. It took the sculptor, Michelangelo, two years to complete.

The leather strap in David's left hand is actually a sling: an ancient weapon used to hurl stones. He uses it to defeat his more powerful opponent.

If you peer between the loosely curling fingers of David's right hand, you can see an object inside. But what is it?

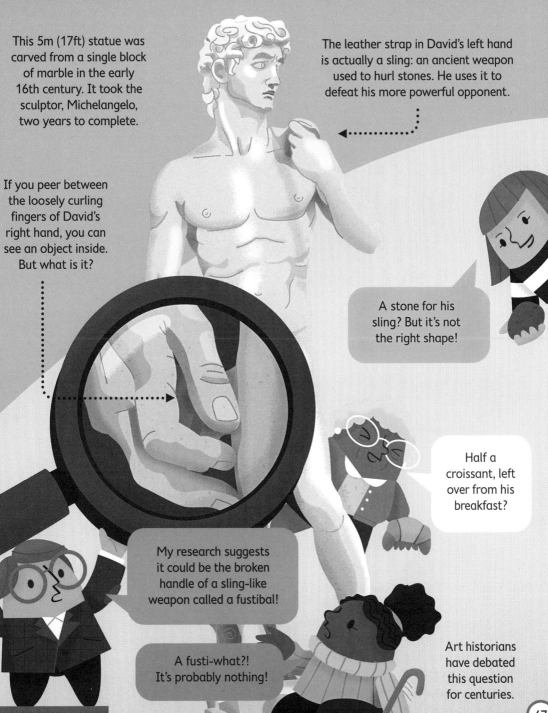

A stone for his sling? But it's not the right shape!

Half a croissant, left over from his breakfast?

My research suggests it could be the broken handle of a sling-like weapon called a fustibal!

A fusti-what?! It's probably nothing!

Art historians have debated this question for centuries.

37 Earth's most ancient tree...

leads a hidden life.

Somewhere up on the slopes of the White Mountains of California grows one of the oldest trees in the world.

It's a type of tree called a **bristlecone pine**.

Bristlecones grow veeeeery slowly.

So slowly, in fact, that a small tree 41cm (16in) in diameter may actually be over 200 years old.

By taking samples from the trunk and counting the rings, scientists have worked out that this particular tree has been growing for nearly **5,000 years**.

It's older than the pyramids of Ancient Egypt.

This ancient tree is so special, the US Forest Service has never revealed its location – nor released any photographs of it. That way, people won't damage it, or disturb its habitat. For the tree's safety, it's a closely guarded secret.

38 Invisible messages...

were written in urine.

Long ago, Roman spies fooled their enemies by adding secret messages to official documents — messages you could *only* find if you already *knew* they were there.

The messages were written in urine. It is slightly acidic, and this would alter the paper... *invisibly*.

When heated up, the altered sections of paper would turn brown... and the message would appear.

39 A star performer's songs...

held top-secret notes.

In the 1940s, German troops occupied France. Little did they know, an American singer and dancer was using her celebrity status to spy on them.

Josephine Baker was invited to lots of important parties throughout Europe, where she spied on German enemy officials for the French Resistance.

After the war, Baker was awarded two of France's highest military awards and could finally reveal her daring double life.

Baker carried sheets of music with her. She covered them with secret messages written in invisible ink — revealing, for example, the location of German troops.

Easter Island's statues walked...

to the place where they stand today.

Out in the Pacific Ocean, far from any other land, lies a speck of volcanic rock and earth known as Easter Island, or Rapa Nui. And all around its coast stand enormous human figures carved from solid stone. The question is, *how did they get there?*

Rapa Nui has over 900 of these statues, known as **moai**. They were made more than 500 years ago — before the islanders had any heavy machinery...

...so how did they move the statues over the long distances from the quarries where they were carved to the coast where they stood?

Number 196 is ready to go!

There are no written records to answer this question, and historians have proposed various theories over the years.

Theory 1: Hauling?
Problem: Takes way too many people.

It's not budging!

Theory 2: Rolling on logs?
Problem: Moai would crush the logs. And there aren't enough trees on Rapa Nui!

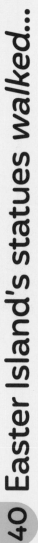

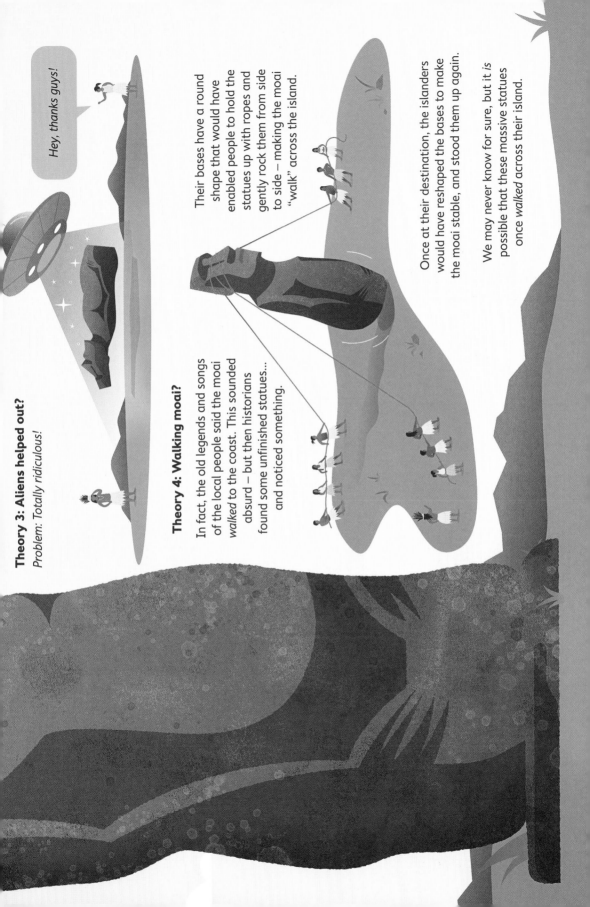

Theory 3: Aliens helped out?
Problem: Totally ridiculous!

Hey, thanks guys!

Theory 4: Walking moai?

In fact, the old legends and songs of the local people said the moai *walked* to the coast. This sounded absurd – but then historians found some unfinished statues... and noticed something.

Their bases have a round shape that would have enabled people to hold the statues up with ropes and gently rock them from side to side – making the moai "walk" across the island.

Once at their destination, the islanders would have reshaped the bases to make the moai stable, and stood them up again.

We may never know for sure, but it *is* possible that these massive statues once *walked* across their island.

41 You have a mystery organ...

tucked inside your tummy.

Doctors have been studying the human body for thousands of years and have a detailed understanding of *almost* every inch of it. But one part, your **appendix**, remains a mystery...

An organ is a part of your body that does a particular job. Scientists don't agree on how many you have – but the most common estimate is 79. Here are some of the main ones.

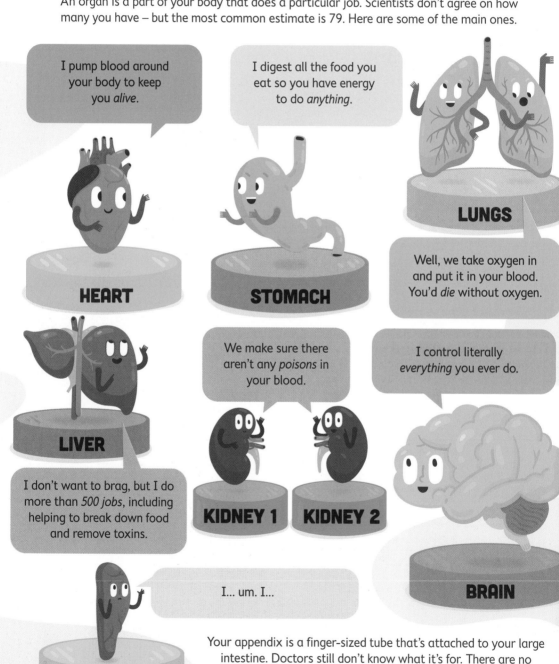

I pump blood around your body to keep you *alive*.

HEART

I digest all the food you eat so you have energy to do *anything*.

STOMACH

LUNGS

Well, we take oxygen in and put it in your blood. You'd *die* without oxygen.

I don't want to brag, but I do more than *500 jobs*, including helping to break down food and remove toxins.

LIVER

We make sure there aren't any *poisons* in your blood.

KIDNEY 1   **KIDNEY 2**

I control literally *everything* you ever do.

BRAIN

I... um. I...

APPENDIX

Your appendix is a finger-sized tube that's attached to your large intestine. Doctors still don't know what it's for. There are no effects if you have it removed. Maybe it doesn't have a job at all?

42 Surviving space travel...

is a race against time.

Human bodies have evolved to function in a very specific environment: Earth. So when they go to space, things eventually start to go wrong...

Astronauts working on the International Space Station (ISS) typically spend about six months at a time in space. From day one, living in **zero-gravity** starts to affect their bodies, and they are bombarded by **cosmic radiation**.

Effects of six months in zero-gravity:

Up to **20%** loss of muscle mass

Up to **10%** loss of bone density

Heart shrinks by up to **18g (0.6oz)**

Spine stretches up to **5cm (2in)**

A range of eye problems

Radiation exposure per day on Earth:

Effects of radiation: various kinds of sickness, eye damage, cancer, even changes to DNA

Radiation exposure per day on the ISS:
250 times more than on Earth

Space agencies are already planning future journeys to Mars. A round-trip would take about 18 months...

Radiation exposure per day on a journey to Mars:
700 times more than on Earth

Currently, astronauts wouldn't survive the round-trip to Mars. The future of space exploration depends on scientists finding ways for humans to survive not just for months, but for *years and years* – and in the face of dangers we don't even know about yet.

43 A made-up disease...

saved lots of lives.

In 1943, a doctor named Giovanni Borromeo was working at a hospital in Rome. According to his records, he had a ward full of patients – all with a previously unknown, contagious disease that he called **Syndrome K**.

At the time, Europe was in the midst of the Second World War. The leader of Nazi Germany, Adolf Hitler, was rounding up Jewish people in Germany and across Europe.

Borromeo took in Jews who were fleeing the Nazis.

He gave them beds in a quarantine ward.

DANGER DO NOT ENTER

Warning: Highly contagious

Causes paralysis and disfiguration

I wrote in all my medical records that they were suffering from an illness called Syndrome K.

QUARANTINE ZONE

When Hitler's soldiers raided the hospital looking for Jews, Borromeo offered to let them search the ward...

...but they were scared they might catch the illness, so refused and left.

And so the Jews stayed safe. Borromeo kept this up until the end of the War in 1945. Historians think he probably saved hundreds of lives. The Nazis never found out that Syndrome K didn't exist.

44 A missing planet...

may have shaped our solar system.

Astronomers have long struggled to explain how the eight planets ended up in their current orbits around the Sun. They all formed close to the Sun – but then *something* scattered them farther out into space.

Mercury

Venus

One possibility astronomers have long considered is that there was once a *ninth* planet in the solar system: a big one, that caused a big incident – and then vanished.

Earth

Mars

That planet would have orbited near the Sun with the others. Then, at some point, it came too close to Jupiter.

Jupiter

Jupiter's powerful gravity wrenched it off course. In a slow chain reaction of mass and momentum, orbits shifted, planets scattered...

Saturn

...and the nameless planet was flung right out of the solar system.

The unnamed planet then became a **rogue planet**: one that doesn't orbit a star, but sails freely through space.

Uranus

No one will ever *see* the missing planet. But astronomers' calculations suggest that billions of years ago, it *may* have been a central piece of our solar system.

Neptune

45 The case of the mummy king...

may never be solved.

When the hidden tomb of an ancient Egyptian king was discovered in 1922, archaeologists quickly saw they had a mystery on their hands. What – or *who* – had killed this young ruler?

KEY EVIDENCE

✓ TUTANKHAMUN'S TOMB WAS UNUSUALLY SMALL FOR A RULER. WAS IT BUILT FOR SOMEONE ELSE?

✓ TUTANKHAMUN WAS FOUND IN A CRAMPED, SECOND-HAND COFFIN.

✓ THE PAINT ON THE WALLS WAS STILL WET WHEN THE TOMB WAS SEALED SHUT.

THE VICTIM

NAME: TUTANKHAMUN
JOB: PHARAOH (KING)
AGE: 19 YEARS OLD
DIED: 1324 BCE
CAUSE OF DEATH:

UNKNOWN

WHAT THE EVIDENCE SHOWS:

TUTANKHAMUN'S DEATH MUST HAVE BEEN ABRUPT AND UNEXPECTED. MOST PHARAOHS HAD LAVISH BURIALS, BUT THIS ONE WAS CLEARLY RUSHED.

1

2

3

HOW DID HE DIE?

AFTER A CENTURY OF EXAMINING THE EVIDENCE, EXPERTS STILL HAVE THREE MAIN THEORIES.

THE YOUNG KING'S KNEE AND THIGH BONE WERE BADLY BROKEN AT THE TIME OF HIS DEATH.

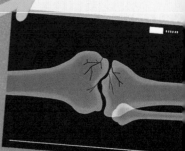

TUTANKHAMUN HAD ONE DEFORMED FOOT THAT IS LIKELY TO HAVE MADE LIFE DIFFICULT.

MEDICAL TESTS SHOWED THAT TUTANKHAMUN HAD A DISEASE CALLED MALARIA IN HIS BLOOD, ANOTHER DISEASE IN HIS BONES, AND A CONDITION CALLED EPILEPSY, WHICH WOULD HAVE GIVEN HIM SEIZURES.

CAUSE OF DEATH: ILLNESS?

IT'S POSSIBLE THAT ONE OR MORE OF THESE CONDITIONS CAUSED THE KING TO WEAKEN RAPIDLY AND DIE...

HIS TOMB HELD A COLLECTION OF 130 WALKING STICKS.

...OR A SUDDEN SEIZURE COULD HAVE CAUSED A FATAL FALL OR A BROKEN BONE THAT MIGHT HAVE LED TO AN INFECTION THAT KILLED HIM.

PAINTINGS OFTEN SHOW TUTANKHAMUN RIDING OR HUNTING.

CAUSE OF DEATH: ACCIDENT?

WAS TUTANKHAMUN KILLED AS A RESULT OF A CHARIOT CRASH?

OR DID HE DIE IN A HIPPO HUNTING ACCIDENT?

SIX CHARIOTS WERE FOUND BURIED IN THE TOMB.

TUTANKHAMUN'S HEART IS MYSTERIOUSLY MISSING FROM HIS BODY.

MISSING!

THE KING WHO CAME AFTER TUTANKHAMUN HAD TUTANKHAMUN'S NAME ERASED FROM THE ROYAL RECORDS.

CAUSE OF DEATH: MURDER?

THE NEXT KING AFTER TUTANKHAMUN WAS A MAN CALLED AY – FORMERLY HIS TRUSTED CHIEF ADVISOR.

WAS THIS A SIMPLE CASE OF BETRAYAL AND MURDER?

46 Unicorns were real...

until 1748.

In 1735, a Swedish biologist named Carl Linnaeus published a book called the *Systema Naturae*. It was the first attempt to make a list of every living thing, and was a turning point in scientific understanding of the natural world. But the first list contained a few unexpected creatures...

His list classified living things into distinct groups, based on what they looked like and how they lived.

The first versions included a group – the Paradoxa – made up of mysterious creatures Linnaeus hadn't seen, but had only heard of. This included a mysterious horse-like creature with a single horn – the unicorn.

Fig. 2

Fig. 1

Fig. 3

Fig. 4

The Paradoxa
1 - Monoceros, or unicorn   3 - Draco, or dragon
2 - Phoenix   4 - Hydra

Linnaeus wanted his list to be thorough, so he included these creatures, based on explorers' drawings and stories. But, over the years, scientists explored more widely. Understanding of the world's wildlife expanded, but no evidence of creatures in the Paradoxa group was ever found. By the sixth printing, in 1748, the unicorn and Paradoxa had been removed.

47 A flame burns to remember...

the soldiers that no one can name.

Every evening, as darkness falls in Paris, a torch is lit. Beneath the flickering flames lie the remains of one unidentified French soldier. This monument is called the **Tomb of the Unknown Soldier**.

There are Tombs of Unknown Soldiers in over 50 countries around the world.

The first was thought to be built in Korea in the 1500s.

The Serbian tomb is built on top of a mountain.

In Harare, Zimbabwe, a flame burns all day every day atop a huge tower, that can be seen from most of the city.

The tomb in Arlington, US, has living quarters beneath it. Guards sleep below it, and don't leave the monument for months at a time.

The tombs usually contain the body of one randomly selected, unidentified soldier. That one represents every soldier that died anonymously.

48 Sharing a secret message...
might keep it private.

Imagine you want to send a secret message. If you use a sneaky code with jumbled-up letters or strings of numbers, this might draw the attention of nosy people. So what if you just... hide it in plain sight?

Hey! What's up? Can I send you a secret message?

Oooh yeah, show me what you've got!

Awww so cute!!

Wait — you're just showing off your cat again! Where's the message?

Sounds like someone hasn't heard of steganography.

Stega-what? Isn't that a dinosaur...?

Steganography! It's the art of hiding secret messages in ordinary items or computer files. This way, only someone expecting a message will know to look for it.

You mean there's a message hidden in the cat picture?!

Yep, it's actually super easy to hide text in a picture.

So, digital images are made up of dots called pixels. By using a computer program, someone writing a secret message can slightly change the shade of certain pixels in the image.

The changes can be so small that a human might not spot them... but a computer could.

The correct computer program can translate the specific shade of particular pixels into letters — and so read the hidden message.

Here, I'll point out the changed pixels for you.

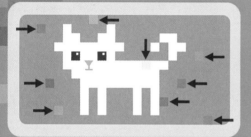

Anyone spying on us could see this image — but only *you* would know to use our steganography program to unravel the message.

Hmm... let me see what I can find...

My computer's got something! Is this it?

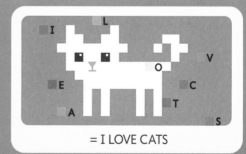

= I LOVE CATS

I already *knew* that! You didn't need a secret message to tell me...

are all that remain of the ancient Mayan libraries.

For over 2,000 years, the Maya people lived and ruled in Central America. They built roads, cities and astronomical observatories, and wrote *thousands* of books. Then, in 1517, Spanish invaders arrived.

The Spanish conquered and took control of their cities. They forced thousands of people to convert to Spain's Catholic religion.

And, to stamp out the Maya's own beliefs and traditions, Spanish priests *burned* all the Mayan books.

We know that the Maya wrote about history, astronomy and mythology. But did they write poetry? Did they write jokes? Or murder mysteries?

These questions will probably remain unanswered. Today, just *four* Mayan books survive.

50 A secret script...

gave women a voice.

For hundreds of years, women living in part of China's Hunan Province communicated with each other using Nüshu: a coded writing that they never taught to men, and which men could not read.

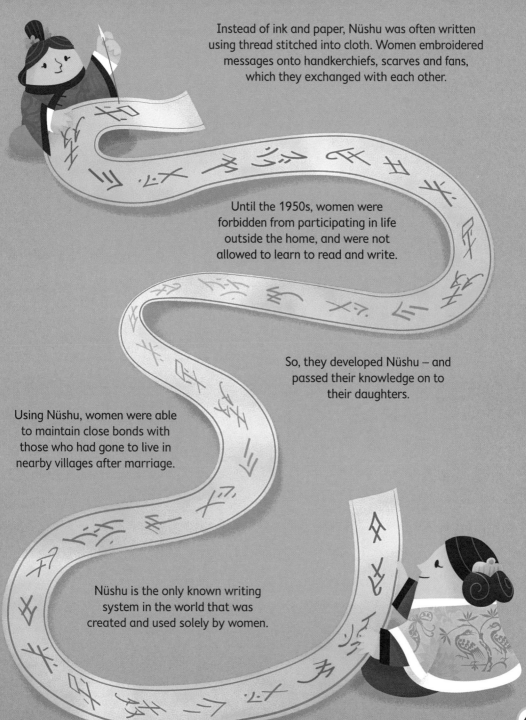

Instead of ink and paper, Nüshu was often written using thread stitched into cloth. Women embroidered messages onto handkerchiefs, scarves and fans, which they exchanged with each other.

Until the 1950s, women were forbidden from participating in life outside the home, and were not allowed to learn to read and write.

So, they developed Nüshu – and passed their knowledge on to their daughters.

Using Nüshu, women were able to maintain close bonds with those who had gone to live in nearby villages after marriage.

Nüshu is the only known writing system in the world that was created and used solely by women.

51 Secret diaries...

reveal the life stories that are often left out of history.

Much of the history that's recorded in books focuses on public events and powerful people. But the stories of people who *didn't* have power – people whose existence wasn't considered important at the time – are harder to study, and often remain unknown.

Luckily, these people could sometimes speak for themselves in their personal diaries.

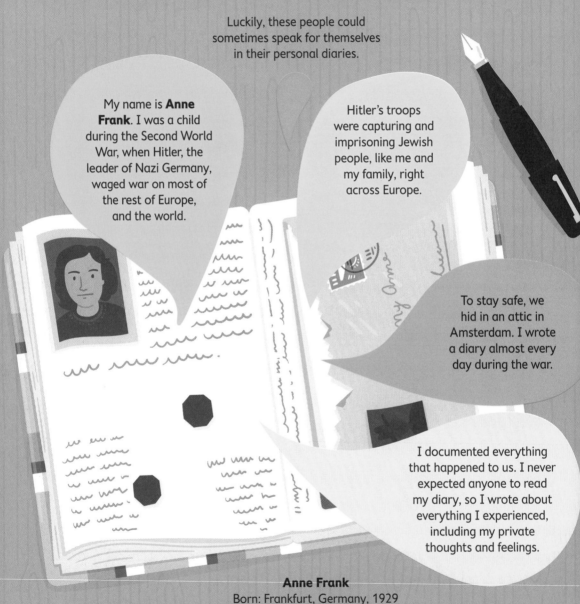

My name is **Anne Frank**. I was a child during the Second World War, when Hitler, the leader of Nazi Germany, waged war on most of the rest of Europe, and the world.

Hitler's troops were capturing and imprisoning Jewish people, like me and my family, right across Europe.

To stay safe, we hid in an attic in Amsterdam. I wrote a diary almost every day during the war.

I documented everything that happened to us. I never expected anyone to read my diary, so I wrote about everything I experienced, including my private thoughts and feelings.

Anne Frank
Born: Frankfurt, Germany, 1929

In 1944, Anne and her family were found and captured by the Nazis. They were held in terrible conditions in a camp where Anne died, at age 15. In total, the Nazis killed approximately six million Jews – around two thirds of all the Jews in Europe. Many Jewish stories and experiences were lost – which makes Anne's diary even more remarkable.

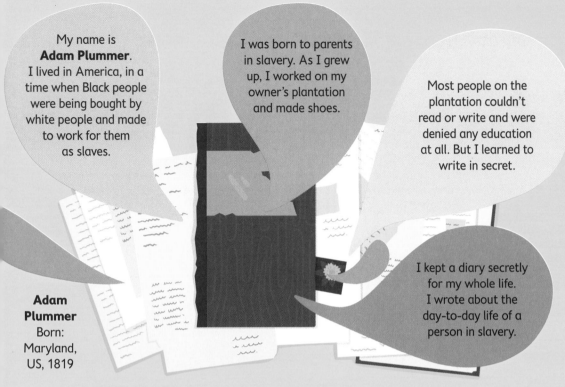

My name is **Adam Plummer**. I lived in America, in a time when Black people were being bought by white people and made to work for them as slaves.

I was born to parents in slavery. As I grew up, I worked on my owner's plantation and made shoes.

Most people on the plantation couldn't read or write and were denied any education at all. But I learned to write in secret.

I kept a diary secretly for my whole life. I wrote about the day-to-day life of a person in slavery.

Adam Plummer
Born: Maryland, US, 1819

This diary was only found in 2003 – almost 200 years after it was written. It is one of just a handful of existing diaries that were written by enslaved people.

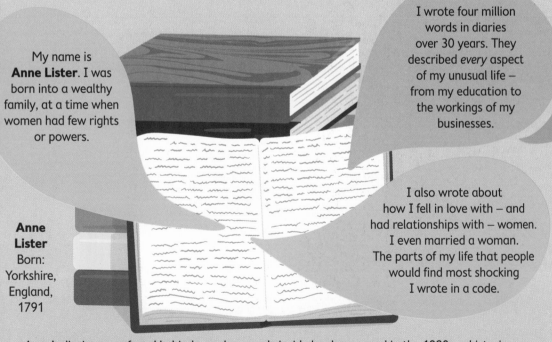

My name is **Anne Lister**. I was born into a wealthy family, at a time when women had few rights or powers.

I wrote four million words in diaries over 30 years. They described *every* aspect of my unusual life – from my education to the workings of my businesses.

I also wrote about how I fell in love with – and had relationships with – women. I even married a woman. The parts of my life that people would find most shocking I wrote in a code.

Anne Lister
Born: Yorkshire, England, 1791

Anne's diaries were found behind wooden panels inside her house, and in the 1980s, a historian began the painstaking work of deciphering the code. Very few historical documents from her time tell the story of women like Anne, but her diaries prove that people like her did exist.

52 An emperor's earlobes...

hold a clue to an ancient question.

In the year 138, the Roman emperor Hadrian died suddenly, at age 62. For nearly 2,000 years, the cause of his death remained a mystery – that is, until 1980, when an American doctor wandered into a museum...

As the doctor examined an ancient sculpture of Hadrian's head, he noticed something on its earlobes: a diagonal crease, or wrinkle, known to modern doctors as **Frank's sign**.

People with this particular earlobe crease are significantly more likely to suffer from certain types of heart disease.

Modern doctors know how they might treat a patient when they spot Frank's sign, but Roman doctors wouldn't have known to look for it.

ROMAN EMPEROR
CAESAR TRAIANUS
HADRIANUS
76 -138 CE

Several portraits of Hadrian – made while he was still alive – show his creased earlobes. This makes it likely that he did indeed have Frank's sign, and offers a new clue to his early death.

53 Beyond red and violet...

is a world that humans cannot see.

Light travels in waves of varying lengths that humans see as a range, or **spectrum**, from red to violet. But there's actually more to the spectrum than we can see. Wavelengths known as **infrared** (IR) and **ultraviolet** (UV) are invisible to us, but *can* be seen by other creatures.

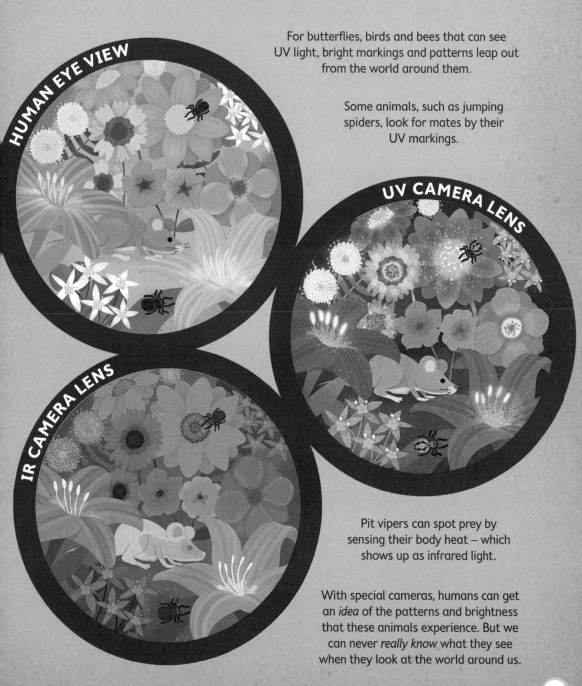

For butterflies, birds and bees that can see UV light, bright markings and patterns leap out from the world around them.

Some animals, such as jumping spiders, look for mates by their UV markings.

HUMAN EYE VIEW

UV CAMERA LENS

IR CAMERA LENS

Pit vipers can spot prey by sensing their body heat — which shows up as infrared light.

With special cameras, humans can get an *idea* of the patterns and brightness that these animals experience. But we can never *really know* what they see when they look at the world around us.

than other infinities.

In mathematics, infinity is the idea that you can count on and on, forever. But there are many different *kinds* of infinity, and although they all go on *until the end of time*, they don't appear to be equally long.

Take this list below, for example, of whole, positive numbers, from one to infinity. It would be *incredibly* long.

But if you include negative numbers along with positive numbers, you get a list that's in theory *twice* as long.

1	1
2	-1
3	2
4	-2
5	3
6	-3
7	4
8	-4
9	5
10	-5
11	6
12	-6
13	7
14	-7
15	8
16	-8
17	9
18	-9
19	10
20	-10
21	11
22	-11
23	12
24	-12

Wait a minute – *both* of these lists would take *forever* to write. So, aren't they both the same size?

We'll never really know how long infinity is. That's the point – it goes on and on and on and on...

55 Mapmakers are baffled...

by medieval sailing charts.

Before the 1200s, maps were just decorative – you couldn't actually use them to navigate. Then, someone began creating surprisingly detailed, useful sailing charts of the Mediterranean Sea. In fact, these are so accurate that modern mapmakers can't figure out how they were made.

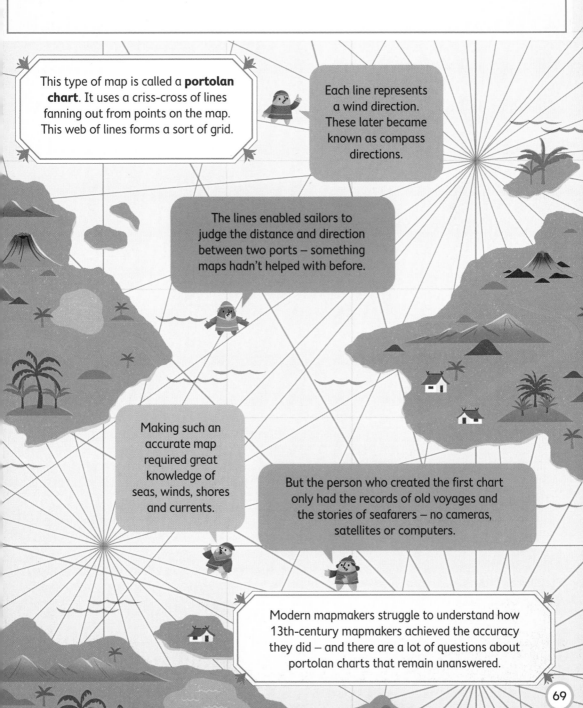

This type of map is called a **portolan chart**. It uses a criss-cross of lines fanning out from points on the map. This web of lines forms a sort of grid.

Each line represents a wind direction. These later became known as compass directions.

The lines enabled sailors to judge the distance and direction between two ports – something maps hadn't helped with before.

Making such an accurate map required great knowledge of seas, winds, shores and currents.

But the person who created the first chart only had the records of old voyages and the stories of seafarers – no cameras, satellites or computers.

Modern mapmakers struggle to understand how 13th-century mapmakers achieved the accuracy they did – and there are a lot of questions about portolan charts that remain unanswered.

56 Floating lights...

aren't as mysterious as they seem.

For hundreds of years, people have reported seeing strange, wispy lights floating above bogs and marshes. They flicker and drift like living things, luring people off paths into dense woods and dangerous swamps.

Around the world, these troublesome creatures have earned themselves lots of different names. Almost every region that has swamps, has a name for them.

Will o' the wisp, in Britain

Ignis fatuus (Latin for foolish fire)

Hinkypunk, in Britain

Aarnivalkea, in Finland

Min Min, in Australia

Aleya, in West Bengal, India

Spunkie, in Scotland

Luz mala (evil light), in Argentina and Uruguay

Chir Batti, in India

Feu follet (marsh fire), in Louisiana, US

Luces del tesoro (treasure lights), in Mexico

Dwaallicht (wandering light), in the Netherlands

Scientists now know that these flickering lights aren't creatures, but are the product of a rare chemical reaction.

Swamps are damp areas where vegetation often rots in water. As it does, it releases different gases – methane, phosphine and diphosphine.

When these gases react with oxygen in the air, they briefly catch fire and glow, like little floating balls of flame.

Some places where these lights appear regularly have become tourist attractions. It seems that understanding what causes these strange phenomena doesn't necessarily stop people from finding them weird and spooky...

57 Museums keep under wraps...

many more treasures than they have on display.

Museums and galleries aren't only places you can visit to look at artifacts. They're places where precious, valuable or just plain interesting objects are stored, preserved and studied. The biggest collections are so vast, only a small percentage is on display.

The British Museum
in London has a collection of around

8 million

objects, and welcomes

6 million

visitors in a typical year.

But only around

1%

of the collection
is on public display.

74%

of the British Museum's
collection is held in
deep storage.

Some of the objects
not on display are
available to view
online...

...but others
might not have
been seen for
decades.

The numbers are similar for other major museums and galleries around the world.

The **Louvre** in Paris shows around **8%** of its vast collection.

The **Hermitage** in St. Petersburg shows around **5%**.

The **Smithsonian Institution** based in Washington D.C. shows less than **1%**.

A further
25%
is available for researchers to study.

In fact, some museums are so old, and have such vast collections, that they don't yet have complete lists of everything they hold.

Who knows what treasures may be hidden in the deepest vaults around the world, waiting to be rediscovered!

58 No one alive today...

can read this message.

In 1999, road workers in Mexico dug up an ancient stone tablet with 62 symbols carved into it. Some resemble plants and animals, others are more mysterious. So far, no one has been able to decipher their meaning, and it may remain that way forever.

This tablet – called the Cascajal block – is nearly 3,000 years old. It was made by people from the ancient Olmec civilization.

These symbols are the oldest writing discovered in the Americas so far. At least, we *think* they're writing! They are arranged in rows and some are repeated – just as in many other written languages.

Similar symbols have been found on other Olmec objects. We just don't know what they mean.

59 Uncovering hidden life...

could expose it to danger.

Scientists are drilling into a lake beneath Antarctic ice. But *should* they?

Eastern Antarctica: under a sheet of ice 4km (2.5 miles) thick lies one of the world's largest lakes. It's called **Lake Vostok**.

Scientists have studied the lake using satellites and radar. Now, to search for life, they need to **drill down** and collect water samples.

The lake has been sealed off and protected by ice for around **15 million years** – so it *may* contain hidden life forms unlike any others on Earth.

But drilling through ice this deep is hard. Drilling teams often use harsh chemicals to stop the borehole from freezing shut.

Those chemicals could leak out into the ice, and then into the untouched waters of the lake. This could endanger anything living down there.

People first began drilling for samples at Lake Vostok in 1998... but scientists still debate whether it's worth risking the lake to discover its secrets. In the search for knowledge, are some questions better left unanswered?

60 It took nearly a century...

for scientists to believe in the platypus.

In 1789, European scientists first set eyes on a stuffed platypus. It seemed so alien and bizarre that they were *sure* it was really an elaborate hoax. In fact, they thought it was probably several animals stitched together.

In the wild, platypuses are only found in Australia – a region totally unfamiliar to most European scientists at the time.

So they were utterly flummoxed when a stuffed platypus arrived in England, and they were faced with an animal that had...

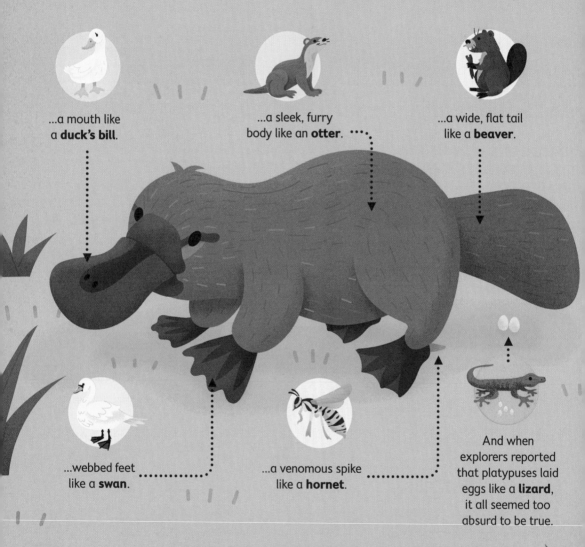

...a mouth like a **duck's bill**.

...a sleek, furry body like an **otter**.

...a wide, flat tail like a **beaver**.

...webbed feet like a **swan**.

...a venomous spike like a **hornet**.

And when explorers reported that platypuses laid eggs like a **lizard**, it all seemed too absurd to be true.

Of course, native people in Australia knew all about the platypus. But it took a long time for European scientists to catch up with them. In fact, it took a century of research and debate before they accepted that the platypus *does* exist.

61 *The Mystery of Edwin Drood...*

was never finished, and will never be solved.

Charles Dickens was a famous English writer, whose last novel tells of a carefree young man who vanishes on a dark and stormy night.

Dickens published books little by little, a few chapters at a time. As a result, readers could be halfway through a novel *before* he had finished writing it.

The Mystery of Edwin Drood was meant to have 12 parts. But, in 1870, after completing just *six*, Dickens fell ill and died.

He didn't leave any notes to reveal how the story was going to end – so generations of readers have been left with the ultimate cliffhanger.

Wait, where is the rest of the story?!

Was Edwin murdered by his wicked uncle, Jasper?

What becomes of Rosa Bud, his former fiancée?

Who is the mysterious stranger who arrives in part five?

What lies in the pit beneath the ancient cathedral?

Despite all these questions, the true fate of Edwin Drood will *forever* be unknown.

62 A vast empire...

vanished into the jungle.

For over 600 years, much of Southeast Asia was ruled by the **Khmer Empire**. At the empire's height, its capital, **Greater Angkor**, was the biggest city in the world. But after 1431, records of the empire just... stop.

For centuries, jungle grew over the former empire, and it was largely forgotten. All that remained were a few spectacular buildings, such as this temple: **Angkor Wat**, in **Cambodia**.

War?

In 1431, the last written record of the empire describes an invasion by the Thai kingdom of Ayutthaya. The city of Angkor was attacked and destroyed. Was the empire finally conquered?

Overpopulation?

The empire covered most of mainland Southeast Asia. Each of its huge cities was packed with people. Were there just too *many* people to feed and provide for?

Then, in 2015, archaeologists flew over the jungle in helicopters equipped with new, laser-mapping tools. Their lasers pierced the dense forest canopy to reveal an *enormous* system of roads and 1,200 square km (460 square miles) of canals.

Beneath the leaves and vines lay a city, Greater Angkor, that's about the same size as Los Angeles today.

So *why* did this once-powerful capital fall into ruin?

Scientists and historians are investigating what caused the empire to collapse. So far, they have lots of questions, but no definitive answer.

Drought?
Tree scientists who studied the rings of ancient trees in Cambodia found evidence of yearly droughts throughout the 14th century. Did the empire's canals and reservoirs start to run dry?

Overfarming?
Earth scientists studied soil samples from a local reservoir. These showed that centuries of overfarming had stripped nutrients from the soil that help crops grow. Did farms start to fail as a result?

63 Four million shells...

line a curious underground grotto.

In 1835, Joshua Newlove and his father were digging a pond in their garden in Margate, England, when they found a hidden, shell-covered cavern. It soon became a popular tourist attraction, but experts still don't know who built it, when or why.

Creating the grotto would have been an enormous task that required lots of people.

Between digging the passageways and transporting the shells to the grotto, experts believe it would have taken *years* to build.

Despite this, no records or stories have been passed through generations that explain its origin.

Gas lamps were used to light the grotto for a long time, but they turned the shells white. Tourists still visit the grotto today and wonder about its origin.

64 People walk in circles...

when they can't tell where they are.

Walking in a straight line *seems* like a simple task. But studies show it's something people find surprisingly tricky when they're lost in the wilderness and bad weather or darkness sets in.

In clear conditions, walkers have little trouble heading straight across unfamiliar landscapes.

But in bad weather...

...they lose track of landmarks...

...veer in different directions...

...and even cross their own paths.

It seems the brain's sense of space and balance isn't completely accurate. Without cues such as landmarks, the Sun or the stars, small errors add up — confusing a person's idea of "straight ahead" so they don't know which way to go and end up going around in circles.

65 Phantom forests...

may or may not exist.

Governments and companies sometimes promise to plant lots of new trees in order to help tackle climate change. But some people call these promised woodlands **phantom forests**, because it's hard to know whether they're ever planted and actually survive...

Sometimes nothing is planted at all.

Sometimes the seedlings are planted but not looked after, so they die.

Sometimes the wrong types of seedlings are planted in the wrong place, and they die.

66 Many mystery microbes...

ride the New York Subway.

Beneath the streets of New York City, there's a train network known as the Subway. Here, scientists have found lots of mysterious microscopic microbes and other life forms.

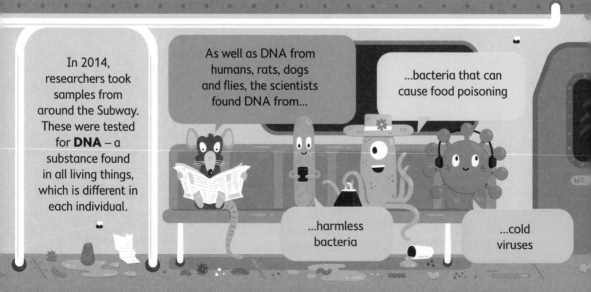

In 2014, researchers took samples from around the Subway. These were tested for **DNA** – a substance found in all living things, which is different in each individual.

As well as DNA from humans, rats, dogs and flies, the scientists found DNA from...

...bacteria that can cause food poisoning

...harmless bacteria

...cold viruses

Sometimes older, existing forests are cut down, in order to plant new seedlings.

But just sometimes, the promise is kept, and a new forest thrives.

In total, the scientists found traces of DNA from more than 15,000 different life forms. They checked these against a vast list: a database of known types of DNA. Almost *half* were unknown.

Some might not have been identified because their DNA hasn't been added to the database yet. BUT many of these mysterious microbes will turn out to be completely new to us.

...bacteria that cause a disease called the bubonic plague (but not enough to infect people)

...a crusty question mark

...a slimy conundrum

...an oozing unknown

...a sticky enigma

67 Roman hair on modern heads...

helped untangle an ancient mystery.

For centuries, historians assumed that the towering, complex hairstyles shown in ancient Roman paintings and statues *couldn't* be made from a person's own hair. Then, a hairdresser decided to investigate.

Professional hairdresser and dedicated historian Janet Stephens was convinced that these elaborate hairstyles weren't just fancy wigs.

Ancient Roman statue

So she studied old Roman texts about fashion and examined artifacts from Roman homes. Then, she took things one step further.

Using only her own skills and the tools available to Romans, she set about recreating the hairstyles on modern women.

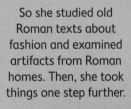

Modern model's head

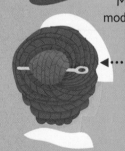

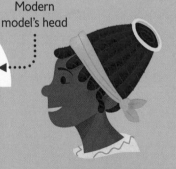

This method of testing ideas about history by trying out ancient techniques and technologies is known as **experimental archaeology**.

In the end, Stephens demonstrated how Romans used combs, ribbons, and even needles and thread to style their hair. Doing so, she helped bring to light a part of women's daily lives that had previously been hidden.

68 Ghost stories...

are as old as literature itself.

The oldest known major work of literature was written down about 4,000 years ago. It's called the *Epic of Gilgamesh*, and features a friendly ghost. Like many other literary ghosts, he tells secrets *no one else* could know.

> I am the spirit of a wild man named Enkidu. In one part of *Gilgamesh*, my friend the king summons me to tell him about the underworld.

> I am the ghost of a king from a play called *Hamlet*. I tell my son, the main character, the truth about my own murder.

> I was once a man named Marley. In *A Christmas Carol*, I warn my business partner, Scrooge, what awaits him in this life – and the next!

The Epic of Gilgamesh

The Tragedy of Hamlet

GHOSTS GALORE

Wuthering Heights

A CHRISTMAS CAROL

Spooks and Spirits

The Lady's Maid's Bell

Ghosts appear in book after book throughout history. Some are frightening and vengeful, some are kind...

...but they often play a similar role: to reveal information that no *living* person could know.

> In a tale by Edith Wharton, I ring a ghostly bell, and lead the way to uncover a secret.

69 The universe is too small...

to contain Graham's number.

In 1971, a mathematician named Ronald Graham was trying to solve a tricky problem. His calculations required a number *so big* that it would be *impossible* for any human brain or calculator to know exactly what it looks like.

Graham's number is so *enormous* that there isn't enough space in the universe to write it down, even if each digit were smaller than a grain of sand.

Uh-oh... I think we're going to need a bigger board!

Even if you could write it down, it would take longer than the age of the universe to do so.

Much bigger!

There are only a few things mathematicians know for sure about Graham's number: it's a whole number, it can be divided by 3 and it ends in 7. But most of the number will always be unknown.

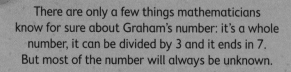

70 A mummy's face may conceal...

pages of long-lost poetry.

In Ancient Egypt, dead people were sometimes turned into mummies before being buried. And *some* mummies were covered with bright decorations, made from scraps of paper with ancient writing on them.

To make mummies, dead bodies were dried in salt and wrapped in cloth. Then, they were often decorated with a painted mask made of a kind of cardboard called **cartonnage**. This cardboard was produced by gluing together many layers of recycled paper.

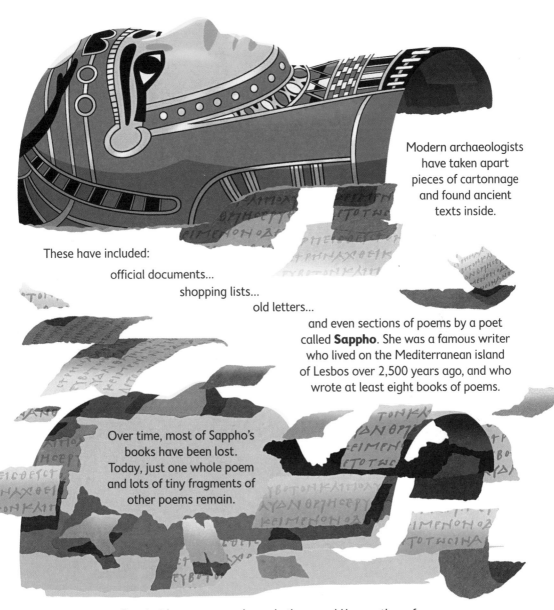

Modern archaeologists have taken apart pieces of cartonnage and found ancient texts inside.

These have included:

official documents...

shopping lists...

old letters...

and even sections of poems by a poet called **Sappho**. She was a famous writer who lived on the Mediterranean island of Lesbos over 2,500 years ago, and who wrote at least eight books of poems.

Over time, most of Sappho's books have been lost. Today, just one whole poem and lots of tiny fragments of other poems remain.

But, inside any mummy's mask, there *could* be another of Sappho's poems, waiting to be discovered. Who knows?

71 Monarch butterflies migrate...

along a route they've never seen before.

Every year, Eastern monarch butterflies set off on a round-trip of almost 10,000km (6,000 miles) in total. But each butterfly only completes *part* of the journey in their lifetime, and there aren't any older butterflies to follow – so how do they know the way?

NORTHEASTERN
US & CANADA
August

FIRST GENERATION
The monarchs that start the journey will cover more than half of the route.

START
SUMMER'S OVER
Time to fly!

UH-OH - STRONG WINDS!
GO BACK **3** SPACES.

September

The *first* generation lives for up to nine months – about eight times longer than most monarchs.

HURRY, IT'S GETTING COLD
Roll again.

Oyamel fir trees

October

CENTRAL
MEXICO
November

MOUNTAINS IN SIGHT
Go forward **1** space.

WINTER BREAK
Huddle for warmth!
Skip a turn.

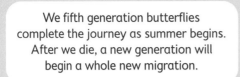
We fifth generation butterflies complete the journey as summer begins. After we die, a new generation will begin a whole new migration.

Milkweed

NORTHEASTERN US & CANADA
June

FIFTH GENERATION TAKES OVER
Switch counter.

May

FINISH MIGRATION COMPLETE!

FOURTH GENERATION TAKES OVER
Switch counter.

April

Scientists think we may use the Sun and the Earth's magnetic field to navigate.

THIRD GENERATION TAKES OVER
Switch counter.

There are no older butterflies to show us the route, but *somehow* we'll find our way!

WARMER WEATHER
Roll again.

TEXAS, US
March

SECOND GENERATION TAKES OVER
Switch counter.

SPRING'S ON ITS WAY
The return journey begins!

TIME TO LAND, LAY EGGS AND DIE
Skip a turn.

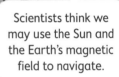

72 *T. rex* keeps getting slower...

and slower.

For decades, the *Tyrannosaurus rex* was thought to be a quick, charging predator – an idea encouraged by action movies. But, in fact, you could probably have easily outwalked a *T. rex*...

Based on *T. rex* bones and fossils, scientists have made computer models to simulate and analyze how these dinosaurs moved.

At first, scientists thought huge, powerful leg bones meant that the *T. rex* would have been a fast runner.

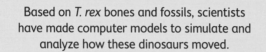

Height: 4m (13ft)

I'm going as fast as I can!

But as computers have developed, the models have become more accurate, and the estimate for the dinosaur's walking speed has got slower...

8km/h (5mph)

7km/h (4mph)

5km/h (3mph)

...and slower.

This is actually at the slow end of average human walking pace. So at a leisurely walk, *you* could have kept up with a plodding *T. rex*.

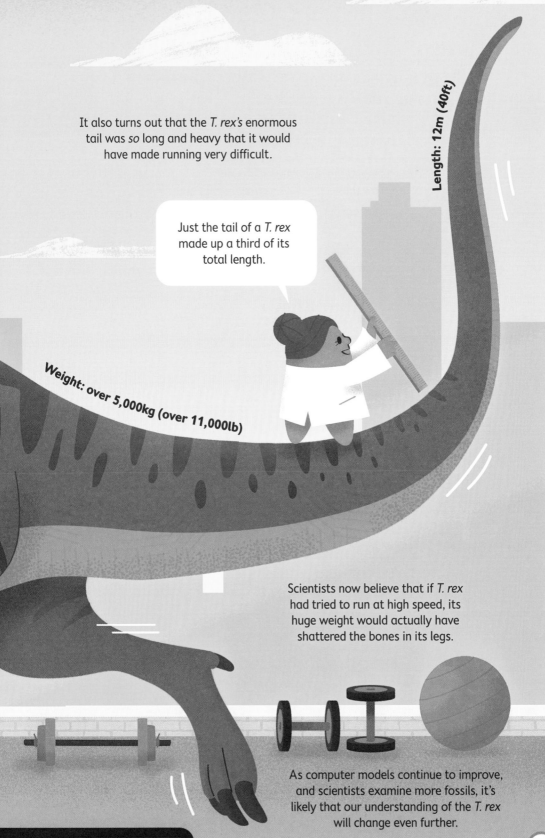

It also turns out that the *T. rex's* enormous tail was *so* long and heavy that it would have made running very difficult.

Just the tail of a *T. rex* made up a third of its total length.

Length: 12m (40ft)

Weight: over 5,000kg (over 11,000lb)

Scientists now believe that if *T. rex* had tried to run at high speed, its huge weight would actually have shattered the bones in its legs.

As computer models continue to improve, and scientists examine more fossils, it's likely that our understanding of the *T. rex* will change even further.

For thousands of years, philosophers and mathematicians have been puzzling over the following statement, known as the **Liar's paradox**.

Is this sentence true... or false?

73 This sentence... is false.

If it's telling the truth, it's false.

Hmm...well if it's false, it's telling us it's true.

I'm not sure we'll ever find the answer.

74 The President's disguise...

requires a fleet of identical helicopters.

Flying by helicopter is a quick and easy way for US Presidents to get around – but it also leaves them vulnerable to attack. To conceal the President's exact location, several identical aircraft fly together.

SPOT THE DIFFERENCE

The answer is... zero differences.
This makes it impossible for anyone to know which helicopter the President is in.

75 No one is allowed to look for...

the lost tomb of Genghis Khan.

Genghis Khan was a ruler from Mongolia who conquered much of China and central Asia, and founded a powerful empire about 800 years ago. He left orders that when he died, his burial place should remain a secret.

There are many legends about how Genghis Khan's tomb was hidden.

Some say that his soldiers killed the workers who built the tomb...

...and galloped 1,000 horses over the spot where he was buried...

...and then killed *themselves* — so no one would be left to reveal Genghis Khan's secret.

Some say the workers changed the course of a river to make it flow over the tomb, hiding it forever.

Some say Genghis Khan was buried on a sacred mountain in Mongolia, in a region which, for hundreds of years, few people were permitted to enter.

In fact, that very mountain is today part of Mongolia's **Khan Khentii Strictly Protected Area**.

In line with Genghis Khan's wish, the government refuses permission for *anyone* to search there for the lost tomb.

76 What a patient doesn't know...
could actually cure them.

Most pills prescribed by doctors contain **active ingredients** – medicines that are proven to ease pain or treat a specific condition. But studies show that sometimes even sugar pills containing *no* active ingredients can help patients.

Contains: SUGAR PILLS [SHOULDN'T work]

Contains: REAL MEDICINE [SHOULD work]

This is known as the **placebo effect**: if a patient *believes* that a fake treatment (a **placebo**) will actually work, then that alone can make the treatment effective.

It's unknown exactly *why* fake medicines work, but researchers have seen many positive effects in patients taking placebos.

If you think that I **DO** work, and I **SHOULD** work, I probably **WILL** work.

If you think that I **DON'T** work, but I **SHOULD** work, I'll probably **STILL** work.

If you think that I **DO** work, even though I **SHOULDN'T** work, I **MIGHT STILL** work.

Perhaps most surprising is that a placebo has been seen to help patients *even if they know* it's a placebo.

If you *know* that I **DON'T** work, and I **SHOULDN'T** work, I *MIGHT STILL* work.

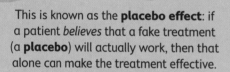

77 Messy handwriting...

means an ancient treasure may be lost forever.

Around 2,000 years ago, a scribe was given the important task of recording the secret locations of hidden treasures – from coins and bowls to huge bars of solid gold – on a scroll made of copper.

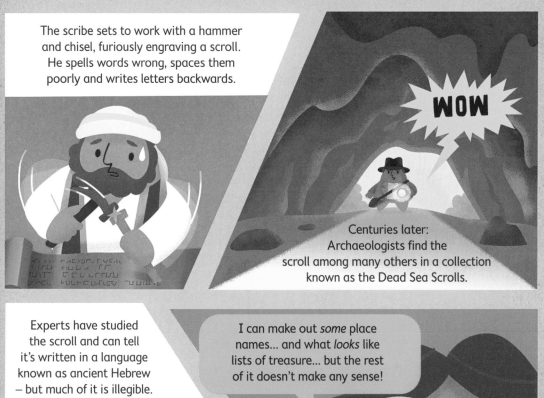

The scribe sets to work with a hammer and chisel, furiously engraving a scroll. He spells words wrong, spaces them poorly and writes letters backwards.

WOW

Centuries later: Archaeologists find the scroll among many others in a collection known as the Dead Sea Scrolls.

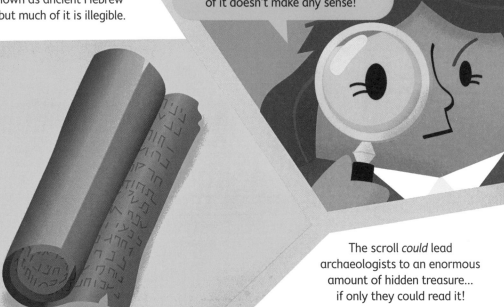

Experts have studied the scroll and can tell it's written in a language known as ancient Hebrew – but much of it is illegible.

I can make out *some* place names... and what *looks* like lists of treasure... but the rest of it doesn't make any sense!

The scroll *could* lead archaeologists to an enormous amount of hidden treasure... if only they could read it!

What do you call things whose names you don't know, or can't quite remember? Around the world, in all languages and dialects, there are *hundreds* of names for half-remembered things.

Doovalacky Australian

Hoojamaflip English

chirimbolo Spanish

Bigyó Hungarian

coSo South American Spanish

Aggeggio Italian

그거 있잖아, 그거 (geugeo issjanh-a geugeo) Korean

Thingamabob

English

Dingsbums

German

Mojäng

Swedish

Huppeldepup

Dutch

なんとかいうやつ

(Nantoka-iuyatsu) Japanese

Be'chi'ngalw

(Beh-chhhh-eeen-gal-loo) Welsh

Machin truc

French

Zamazingo

Turkish

79 Only 4% of the internet...

is easily searchable.

Whenever you search for something online, you're actually scrolling through what scientists call the **surface web**. But *beneath* the surface web is a huge, tangled web of private, secret and illegal information...

**The surface web:
around 4%**

The surface web includes Google, Wikipedia, and everything you can find if you use a search engine.

**The deep web:
around 90%**

Under the surface web is the **deep web**. The deep web hides all sorts of things – from government documents and medical records, to private emails and financial and legal information.

These hidden things aren't *bad* – they're just not things that everyone should have access to all the time.

**The dark web:
around 6%**

The bottom corner of the deep web is called the **dark web**. It's a secretive place that's rife with dangerous and illegal activity.

It's hard to find, and hidden under layers and layers of encryption – a kind of code that locks information away.

80 Roman thingamabobs...

sparked a world-wide guessing game.

Hundreds of twelve-sided bronze objects, called **dodecahedrons**, have been found all over Europe. There's no mention of them in any Roman texts, so archaeologists are trying to figure out exactly *what* they were.

Some people think they were used as dice...

... or as candlesticks...

... or as weights for fishing nets.

Other possible uses include glove makers' finger measurers, fortune-telling tools, or *maybe* astronomical tools used to predict the best time to sow grain.

Archaeologists have mainly found these 2,000-year-old thingamabobs among coins and other treasured objects, so they suspect they were considered valuable. But as to what they were for, we may never know.

81 Revenge is best served...
at a banquet laced with undetectable poisons.

Long ago, people in power used a variety of peculiar objects to protect themselves from food poisoned by rivals – but most of their methods didn't actually work.

Glass goblets from Venice were thought to be so pure that they would shatter if they touched poison.

82 The purpose of yawning...
still has scientists bamboozled.

We all yawn. When you see someone else yawning, you might even start to yawn yourself! But what's it for?

Could it be to cool down the brain when it gets too warm?

Is it to give the lungs a good stretch?

Does the movement bring blood to the brain to wake it up when you're tired or bored?

Might yawning when someone else does be a way to bond and show empathy?

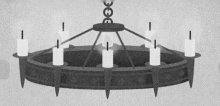

Fossilized shark teeth were sold as dragons' tongues, to purify poison if placed in food.

Opal rings were thought to turn pale in the presence of poison.

Narwhal tusks were made into "unicorn horn" spoons and knives. People believed they changed shade if touched by poison.

Some very unfortunate people were made to taste the feast *before* their masters, to check for poison.

83 Maps of the Moon...

were completed long before maps of the Earth.

In 1966, the first human-made satellite blasted off to orbit the Moon. Just decades later, in 2020, advanced satellites completed a detailed map of its entire surface. *Earth*, however, is proving far more difficult.

The problem is water. Satellites can scan rocky surfaces easily – but they can't see through deep water.

To map mountains, plains and canyons hidden beneath the Earth's oceans, scientists use ships and submarines.

They have to scan one small section at a time. It will take them until 2030 to finish a detailed map.

Moon's surface:
100% mapped!

Earth's surface:
still working on it!
The surface is 70% ocean, you know.

84 Gaps in a grid...

can uncover the building blocks of the universe.

The basic building blocks that make up everything in the universe are called **elements**. Each one has its own properties. In the 1800s, a Russian scientist named Mendeleev tried to make sense of them by arranging them into a grid.

Each element has a different **atomic mass**. Atomic mass means how much stuff is inside each tiny atom of an element – in other words, how heavy it is. Mendeleev listed them from low to high atomic mass.

He divided his list into rows of similar elements – but then he found that there were gaps left over.

B	C	N	O	F
Boron	Carbon	Nitrogen	Oxygen	Fluorine
Al	**Si**	**P**	**S**	**Cl**
Aluminium/ Aluminum	Silicon	Phosphorus	Sulfur/ Sulphur	Chlorine
?	**Ti**	**V**	**Cr**	**Mn**
	Titanium	Vanadium	Chromium	Manganese

> I left these gaps for elements that hadn't been discovered yet. From the patterns in my grid, I could predict the atomic mass and other properties of the undiscovered elements.

? **?**

Br
Bromine

?

> I called this grid the **periodic table**. Scientists still use a version of it today, and have filled in all my gaps!

85 Element 119...

may or may not exist.

Since Mendeleev, scientists have discovered more elements. The modern periodic table contains 118 of them. But is there a 119th?

Some of the 118 elements were very difficult to discover. They weren't found, but *made* in laboratories. They are **radioactive** — which means they start to disappear as soon as they form — so they only exist for fractions of seconds.

Chemists debate whether it's possible to create any more new elements, or whether they might already exist somewhere in the universe.

?

119

To make new elements in a lab, scientists fire tiny particles at an existing element. Sometimes the particles fuse with the element and create a new one.

But to create element 119, the particles would need to be fired so *hard* and so *fast* that they would melt the element, and probably all the equipment too.

Until new technology or a new technique is invented, whether element 119 *could* be made remains unknown.

The greatest ever hoaxes...

have made scientists believe the unbelievable.

A hoax is a trick designed to fool as many people as possible. Often, it doesn't matter how far-fetched a hoax might seem. If people *want* to believe it, even the most sceptical scientists will fall for it.

WE CORDIALLY INVITE
YOU TO VISIT OUR

FANTASTICAL SHOW

INCREDIBLE Hoaxes!

OF

Roll up! Come and see the fabulous "Fiji Mermaid" – an ugly, dried-up specimen!

The mermaid was first shown in London in 1822. Then, showman P.T. Barnum took it on tour in America, where thousands flocked to see

THE FIJI MERMAID

THIS EXTRAORDINARY CREATURE WAS SUPPOSEDLY CAUGHT BY FISHERS OFF THE ISLANDS OF FIJI IN THE SOUTH PACIFIC. IN FACT, IT WAS ONE OF MANY MADE FROM THE UPPER HALF OF A MONKEY SEWN TOGETHER WITH THE TAIL OF A FISH.

MARVEL AT SOME OF THE MOST PREPOSTEROUS DECEPTIONS THAT EVER FOOLED THE WORLD! PLEASE LEAVE ALL DISBELIEF AT THE DOOR.

The Cottingley Fairies

☆ ☆

In 1917, two schoolgirls in the north of England took a series of photos of fairies frolicking in their garden.

A debate raged in national newspapers over whether the pictures were genuine or fakes. Decades later, the girls confessed that the fairies were paper cutouts.

The camera never LIES! Or does it?

WHAT MAKES MYSTERIOUS SIGHTINGS, IMPROBABLE CLAIMS AND BIZARRE BEINGS SO APPEALING TO OTHERWISE RATIONAL PEOPLE? WE MAY NEVER FULLY UNDERSTAND...

THE MECHANICAL AUTOMATON
CHESS PLAYER

From 1770 to 1854, this contraption toured Europe and America, challenging people to play it at chess. It even defeated scientist Benjamin Franklin and French ruler Napoleon Bonaparte, who had no clue there was a chess master crouched in a hidden chamber inside.

Can you tell FACT from FICTION??

87 The future of chocolate spread...

is uncertain.

One of the main ingredients of chocolate spread is actually hazelnuts. But hazelnut trees are being wiped out by infections. Scientists are racing to find a solution – but will they find one before it's too late?

70% of all the hazelnuts in the world are grown in Turkey. Hazelnut trees struggle to grow in other places – the conditions aren't right, and there are diseases in the soil.

But now fungal diseases are threatening hazelnut trees in Turkey too.

WANTED
SUPER RESISTANT HAZELNUT TREES

CHOX

CHOCOLATE SPREAD

Palm oil free

In labs around the world, scientists are testing thousands of hazelnut tree varieties.

NUT HUNT

They think there might be a variety out there somewhere that can resist infections. A race is on to find it.

If they can *find* one, or *breed* one by crossing various species together, they *might* be able to use it to mass-produce hazelnuts again. But until then, the future of chocolate spread is on a knife-edge.

88 The search for life in space...

starts with a quest to find water.

Life, as we know it, thrives on Earth because the conditions are just right. So, astronomers hoping to discover life on *other* planets or moons hunt for places with similar conditions. They don't know whether they'll succeed, but they have a good idea where to start.

Liquid water is vital for life. Earth has lots of it, but a few other places in our solar system have water too:

Mars and Venus

Moons of Jupiter: Europa, Ganymede and possibly Callisto

Moons of Saturn: Enceladus and Titan

Scientists have sent probes to investigate these places, but they haven't found signs of life... *so far*.

Water isn't the *only* condition for life. Using powerful telescopes, astronomers have found over 50 planets in other star systems that appear to have other similarities with Earth:

 ? **?**
They're roughly the same **size**.

They orbit near enough to their star to get its **light** – a source of **energy** that life needs to grow...

They might have an **atmosphere** that can block out harmful radiation from space.

...but not *so* near that they'd burn up.

In 2021 a new telescope was launched into space: the **James Webb Space Telescope**. It's giving astronomers a closer look at far-off planets, and is helping to answer key questions about whether they *could* support life.

Do these planets have rocky surfaces that contain crucial **elements**, including **iron** and **carbon**?

Do they hold any water?

Do the atmospheres on these planets contain life-giving **oxygen**...

...or deadly gases?

Armed with this information, astronomers can decide which planets deserve further study, in the hope of finding life.

89 A pocket camera...

could solve a mountaineering mystery.

On the 8th of June, 1924, two British mountaineers left their tent on the upper slopes of Mount Everest – the world's highest peak. They were hoping to be the first ever to reach the summit. They climbed slowly up into the clouds... and disappeared, never to return.

We know the climbers, George Mallory and Andrew Irvine, perished *somewhere* high on the mountain.

But for decades, people have wondered: did they reach the summit *before* disaster struck?

And there is one missing piece of evidence that *could* settle the question: the **Kodak Vest Pocket Model B**.

This is a small, portable camera carried by the climbers. *If* they reached the summit, they'd probably have used this to take a selfie.

If anyone ever finds this camera, preserved by the snow and frozen mountain air, it *might* contain photos that rewrite the history of mountain climbing.

90 No one knows who really won...

the Battle of Kadesh.

About 3,300 years ago, two powerful armies clashed near the town of Kadesh, in what is now Syria. Historians know lots and lots of details about the battle – but they *don't* know who won the fight.

This was part of a struggle between two rival powers: the Egyptian Empire and the Hittite Empire.

The battle began with a surprise attack by Hittite chariots. They drove straight into our camp!

Up to 5,000 chariots drove into battle, alongside some 60,000 foot soldiers.

At one point our Egyptian ruler, Ramesses II, was surrounded by enemies. He had to fight his way to safety!

There are more records about the Battle of Kadesh than any other ancient conflict, but the records of *both* sides boast of a glorious victory.

To this day it's unclear who really won.

91 A paper lock...

kept secret letters safe from prying eyes.

Imagine it's the late 16th century. You're an English spy in Venice, and you have a secret message for the Queen. It will take weeks for a letter to reach London by sea and land. Sealed envelopes don't exist yet. So, how can you be sure no one will read your message before it arrives?

The answer is **letterlocking**: a sneaky way of sealing letters using just a few simple tools and the letter itself.

Locking a letter makes it *impossible* to open without tearing or cutting it. That way, anyone receiving the letter would *know* if its secrets had been seen by prying eyes.

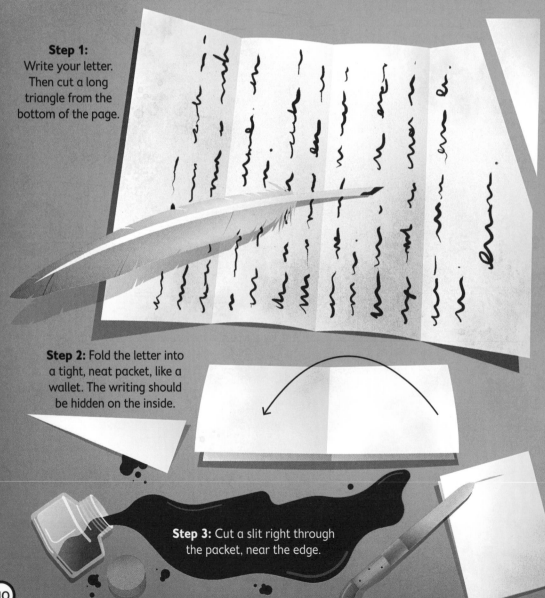

Step 1: Write your letter. Then cut a long triangle from the bottom of the page.

Step 2: Fold the letter into a tight, neat packet, like a wallet. The writing should be hidden on the inside.

Step 3: Cut a slit right through the packet, near the edge.

Step 4: Then stick the narrow, pointed end of the triangle through the slit.

Step 5: Melt a blob of sticky wax onto the tip of the triangle where it comes through the paper. Move quickly on to Step 6!

Step 6: Wrap the wide end of the triangle around the edge of the letter, so that it covers the blob of wax.

Step 7: Use a seal such as this, with a unique symbol, to stamp the wide end of the triangle tightly down onto the wax, sealing the letter.

This simple "triangle lock" is just one of many letterlocking techniques used for centuries by everyone – from merchants to spies to kings and queens...

...for example, on the night before her execution in 1587, Mary, Queen of Scots wrote a final letter to her brother-in-law, the King of France. And when she finished, she locked it.

92 A crooked forest...

has stumped tree experts for decades.

There's a forest in Poland called Kryzwy Las that's filled with pine trees that have grown crooked near the bottom. There are a few theories about how this happened, but one is more likely than others...

MYSTERY GAME SHOW

50,000

25,000

10,000

5,000

1,000

? ?

The trees planted in Kryzwy Las in the 1930s began to grow crooked when they were around ten years old.

What was the *most* likely cause?

A   Army tanks drove over the trees, causing them to grow sideways.

B   Heavy snowfall bent the trees over, making them grow crooked.

C   Farmers bent the trees on purpose so their wood could be used to make ships or furniture.

Well, Barry, no one knows for sure, but option C is most likely! War broke out in Europe and the farmers never finished the job, so the trees kept growing with a crooked curve at the bottom.

93 A cow is a compass...

while it snacks.

Farmers have noticed that cows usually all face in the same direction, either north or south, when they eat. Scientists have studied thousands of grazing cattle around the world, but still can't explain this strange habit.

Scientists have found that cows almost always align themselves along the north-south line, regardless of where they are in the world, their breed or the time of day.

It's possible that cows, like some other animals, can sense Earth's north-south magnetic field and use it to find their way around. But *why* the cows line themselves up in this way is still unknown.

94 The limit of human speed...

is yet to be discovered.

For the last century, sprinters have been getting faster and faster over a distance of 100m. But they're getting faster by smaller and smaller margins. Surely one day, people will reach a limit. But where is that limit?

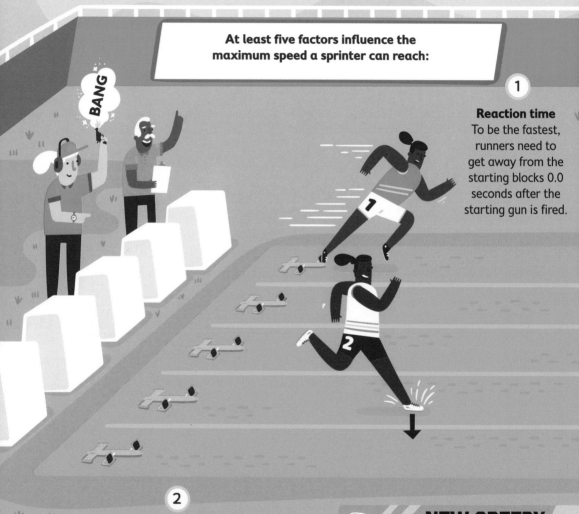

At least five factors influence the maximum speed a sprinter can reach:

1

Reaction time
To be the fastest, runners need to get away from the starting blocks 0.0 seconds after the starting gun is fired.

2

Force through the ground
This is the big one. Scientists think that the amount of force runners push through their foot into the ground is the biggest thing in a runner's control that will affect their speed.

NEW SPEEDY GO-FAST SHOES

To speed up, runners need to put more force into the ground *or* stay on the ground for longer. It might be that new running shoe inventions could help.

Woooo

Cheer!

RUN LIKE THE WIND!

WORLD RECORD!

In 1896, the record for a 100m sprint was 12 seconds. Today, the fastest teenagers can beat that.

By 1968 the record was under 10 seconds.

But since then, the record has only been beaten by half a second – so scientists think we're reaching the limit.

(3)

Drag
Drag is how air around the runners pulls back on them and slows them down. Things such as clothing design and new technical fabrics could reduce drag and help runners speed up.

(4)

The weather
A slight tailwind, blowing from behind, can help – but too much means any records aren't valid.

(5)

Strength, power and build
Might people in the future be taller, and stronger? Diet and training can help, but by how much?

Scientists have run various calculations, and all come out with slightly different predictions about human speed. It's even possible that the record for human speed has *already been set* – but how will we know when the limit has been reached?

95 A magician's secrets...

are protected by The Magic Circle.

Only the best magicians from around the world are selected to join an exclusive society called The Magic Circle. Members meet to refine and share the secrets behind their tricks.

To join the society, magicians must either write a 4,000-word thesis or perform in front of members of the Council.

Our headquarters has a library of magic and a museum filled with props and treasures that tell the story of this century-old society.

We are forbidden to disclose any secrets of magic to anyone other than fellow members, or students of magic.

Members who break the rules of The Magic Circle are expelled.

Members of the public can visit our headquarters to watch us perform.

Elite members can join the top-secret Inner Circle, where they study and create the greatest magic tricks the world has ever seen.

96 The search for a magical stone...

led to real scientific discoveries.

From ancient times until the 17th century, scholars across China, India, Europe and the Middle East, known as **alchemists**, spent their lives seeking a substance known as the **philosophers' stone...**

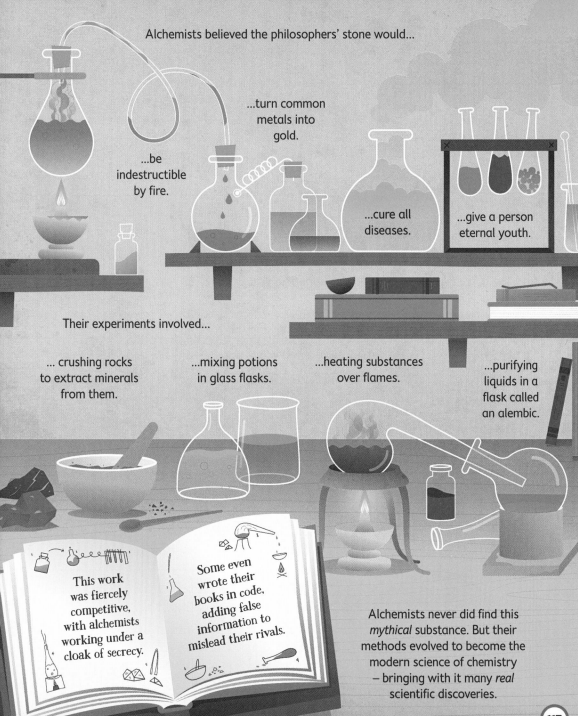

Alchemists believed the philosophers' stone would...

...turn common metals into gold.

...be indestructible by fire.

...cure all diseases.

...give a person eternal youth.

Their experiments involved...

... crushing rocks to extract minerals from them.

...mixing potions in glass flasks.

...heating substances over flames.

...purifying liquids in a flask called an alembic.

This work was fiercely competitive, with alchemists working under a cloak of secrecy.

Some even wrote their books in code, adding false information to mislead their rivals.

Alchemists never did find this *mythical* substance. But their methods evolved to become the modern science of chemistry – bringing with it many *real* scientific discoveries.

97 The hand you write with...

is confusingly unpredictable.

Up to 90% of people in the world are right-handed. Almost everyone else is left-handed. Historians think it's been that way for thousands of years. But no one knows why.

By studying skeletons, tools and cave paintings from many thousands of years ago, historians guess that most prehistoric people were right-handed, but some were left-handed. That's the same as the pattern we see today.

Scientists used to think more people were right-handed because human brains have a left and a right side. But they haven't found a significant difference in the way right- and left-handed people's brains work.

They also thought being right- or left-handed was being passed down in genes. But not all families use the same hand; so this idea doesn't hold up either.

Scientists still *think* there could be *something* being passed down in genes – but there's no clear pattern.

No matter how many studies scientists and doctors do, they can't yet figure out why some people are left-handed, why most people are right-handed, nor even how to predict which hand a child will use.

98 Tuzo and Jason...

are two continent-sized blobs lurking underground.

In the 1970s, earth scientists detected two gigantic, shapeless blobs deep below Earth's surface. Technically they're termed **large low-shear-velocity provinces**, but they also have nicknames: *Tuzo* and *Jason*.

How the blobs were found

Earthquakes send waves of sound down as well as up. Scientists use machines to track these waves as they bend around or pass through different layers of rock.

Seeing soundwaves behave in unusual ways was the first glimpse people had of these mysterious blobs.

Hi, I'm Jason! Scientists detected me deep below the Pacific Ocean.

Hi, I'm Tuzo! I'm down below Africa. I'm less than half the size of Jason, but I'm still ENORMOUS!

Known:

Both blobs sit thousands of miles below the Earth's surface, in a region known as the **lower mantle**.

They move and change shape slowly, a little like blobs of wax in a lava lamp.

They're made of something thicker than the molten rock around them.

They seem to influence volcanic activity above them.

Unknown:

How and when they formed.

What they're made of. They may even be made of substances that don't exist on Earth's surface.

How long they will continue to exist — it may not be forever.

could make you a lot happier.

Knowledge is essential. Without it, we couldn't have science, medicine or any kind of progress. Yet many old sayings known as **proverbs** suggest that, *sometimes*, ignorance – or *not* knowing – can make life easier.

The world is full of disasters – big and small – that you alone can't prepare for, prevent or put right.

Rogue asteroids!

Bad hair days!

Lightning strikes!

Mean comments!

Erupting volcanoes!

You smell!

Doo, doo, da doo!

You smell!

"Not knowing is Buddha" or "What you don't know can't hurt you"
–Japanese proverb

"Ignorance is sweet for the soul"
–Kurdish proverb

"Ignorance is bliss"
–English proverb

"Ignorance is the peace of life"
–Kashmiri proverb

"The less you know, the better you sleep"
–Russian proverb

Would you be better off just... *not* knowing about these things? Could we live with less knowledge and fewer worries?

100 If our civilization ended today...

tomorrow's scientists might think we were *never here*.

Today, much of Earth's surface – covered with cities and roads, vehicles and machinery – appears to be shaped by humans. But, in just a few million years, nearly every trace of our existence could vanish.

Imagine there were no living humans left on the planet.

Wind, rain, forests, floods and earthquakes would quickly break down our structures and objects, and wash them into the oceans.

As dust and mud settled over them, *all* the remains of human activity would be pressed into a layer about 2.5cm (1in) thick.

Plastic, metals, chemicals

Civilization as we know it, with its concrete buildings and mass-produced machinery, has only existed for about **300 years**.

Layers of rock

That's a mere blip in the **400 million years**, give or take, since the first complex, land-based life on Earth.

In all that time, only a *tiny fraction* of plant and animal species have been preserved as fossils. It's possible that *no* human fossils would ever be found.

So, if alien archaeologists visited Earth 100 million years from now, they might logically conclude that human civilization had simply... never existed.

Nope, nothing here! On to the next planet.

The idea that an entire advanced civilization could disappear leaving hardly a trace is known as the **Silurian Hypothesis**.

Where on Earth?

The numbers on this map of the world show the locations of some of the "100 things" described in this book.

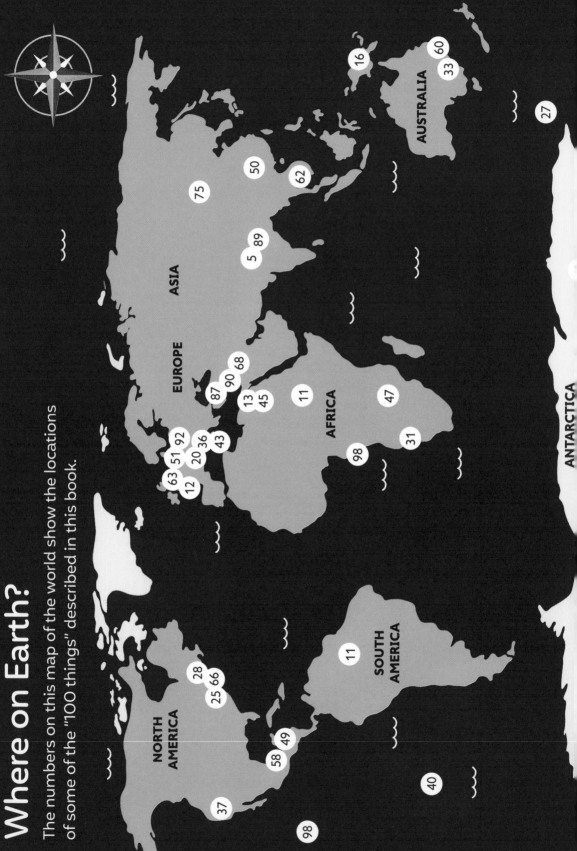

Glossary

This glossary explains some of the words used in this book.
Words written in *italic* type have their own entries.

alchemist Someone, in the past, who attempted to turn common substances into something valuable through a combination of science and superstition

alembic A flask with a beaked head. Formerly used by alchemists to purify substances

anonymous Someone whose name is unknown

archaeologist Someone who learns about the past, often by digging up old objects and studying them

astronomer A scientist who studies space, often using telescopes to detect distant objects

astrophysicist A scientist who studies how stars work

atom An incredibly tiny particle; the smallest building block of an *element*

atomic mass The size of an *atom*

axis An imaginary line through the middle of an object, around which that object spins

bacteria Microscopic living creatures

Big Bang, the A theory about how the *universe* began through the instantaneous appearance and rapid expansion of matter from an infinitesimally small point

bioluminescence The ability of certain living things to make their own light

cell One of trillions of tiny building blocks that make up most living things

comet A ball of ice and dust in space that *orbits* a star

cosmic radiation Potentially dangerous *radiation* that is emitted by stars

cox A member of a rowing crew who does not row, but is in charge of steering the boat

dark energy An unknown, and *hypothetical*, form of energy that produces a force that opposes *gravity* and is causing the *universe* to expand

dark matter An invisible, unknown substance with a strong *gravitational* pull

DNA A complex chemical code found inside *cells* that contains information about the characteristics of a living thing

dodecahedron An object that has twelve faces or sides

elements The basic chemical substances that make up all matter

espionage The use of spies to obtain secret information about the plans or activities of a rival group

experimental archaeology A field of study that tries to learn about the past by experimenting and testing *hypotheses* about how things worked

fossil The remains or trace of a living animal or plant that died long ago, found preserved in earth or rock

fungus One of a large group of living things, including mushrooms, that appear similar to plants

galaxy A collection of billions of stars that *orbit* together around a central hub

generation All of a group of people or animals born and living at the same time

genes Sections of *DNA* that contain a code to define specific characteristics of a living thing, such as height

gravity The force of two objects pulling on each other; the force that keeps Earth in *orbit* around the Sun

habitat The place where an animal or plant *species* lives

hoax A trick or deception

hypothesis A statement or idea that can be tested and used to guide further study

infinity The concept that something is endless, unlimited or goes on forever

International Space Station (ISS) A crewed vessel that *orbits* around the Earth, where astronauts from many countries live and work

internet A vast computer network that enables computer users to connect with one another

koan A story, riddle or statement used in *Zen Buddhism* that has no set meaning

leprosy An infectious disease caused by bacteria

letterlocking The act of folding and securing a written message so it cannot be read without breaking a seal

microbes Microscopic *organisms* such as *bacteria* or viruses

migrate To move from one country or region to another

Nobel Prize A set of prizes awarded each year for important work in science, literature, economics or for world peace

Olmec civilization The earliest major civilization in Central America

Olympic Games An international sports competition held every four years

oneirologist A scientist who studies dreams

orbit To travel through space around another, larger object

organism An individual life form

paradox A statement that is logically unacceptable or contradicts itself – but that may be true

periodic table A table including all 118 known chemical *elements*, grouped according to their *atomic* properties

phantom forest A forest that has failed to come into being either because the trees have died, been cut down, or were never planted at all

placebo A substance that is *not* medicine but is given to someone who is told it *is* medicine

placebo effect When someone's health appears to improve as a result of taking a *placebo*

prime number A number that can only be divided by itself or one

proverb A traditional saying that expresses a widely held belief or useful thought

pseudonym A false name someone uses instead of their real name

pulsar A star that spins very fast and cannot be seen, but that produces huge amounts of *radiation*

radiation Powerful and dangerous energy that comes from the breaking up of *atoms*

radioactive Something that emits *radiation*

reverse engineering The process of studying another company's product to see how it is made, often in order to copy it

rogue planet A planet that doesn't orbit a star but travels freely through space

satellite An object, natural or human-made, that *orbits* a planet

sign language A way of communicating using hand movements

solar system, the The group of planets, moons and asteroids that *orbit* the Sun

species A type of animal, plant or other living thing

sphinx A mythical creature with the head of a human, the body of a lion and the wings of a falcon

steganography A way of hiding secret information or messages in a medium that is not secret

taxonomist A scientist who groups living things into categories

tectonic plates Large pieces of land that make up the Earth's crust

trade secret Something, such as a recipe, process or device, that gives a business or individual an advantage over a competitor

universe Everything in time and space

Zen Buddhism A school of Buddhism – an Asian religion or philosophy – that originated in China

Index

Knowing so little...
took a lot of knowledge.

Research and writing by
Jerome Martin, Alice James,
Micaela Tapsell and Alex Frith

Designed by
Jenny Offley, Lenka Jones
and Tom Ashton-Booth

Additional editorial material by
Lan Cook, Tom Mumbray,
Laura Cowan, Victoria M. Williams
and Amy Chiu

Illustrated by
Federico Mariani, Shaw Nielsen,
Dominique Byron and Geraldine Sy

Ah, I see! The team relied on expert advice from Dr. Samraghni Bonnerjee, Dr. Phoebe Griffith, Dr. Roger Trend, Dr. Daisy Shearer, Dr. Caitriona Cox and Dr. Audrey Curnock

Series editor: Ruth Brocklehurst
Series designer: Stephen Moncrieff

It's amazing how so many people managed not to know so many things!

First published in 2023 by Usborne Publishing Limited, 83-85 Saffron Hill, London EC1N 8RT, United Kingdom. usborne.com